THE

ULTIMATE BODY

BOOK

FOR GIRLS

Everything a Girl Need to Know for Growing Up Happy!

By

KELLY D. TAYLOR

TABLE OF CONTENTS

CHAPTER THREE

FRIENDS AND FEELINGS

CHAPTER FOUR

I DON'T LIKE HOME

CONCLUSION

INTRODUCTION

Welcome to a journey of self-discovery and empowerment! In this book, we will explore the challenges that young girls face in their everyday lives and offer practical solutions to help them overcome them.

Growing up is not always easy. It can be especially difficult for young girls who are navigating through a world that can be both exhilarating and overwhelming.

From dealing with school, friends, family, and their changing bodies, there are many obstacles that can get in the way of their growth and success.

This book is designed to help young girls take charge of their lives and become the best versions of themselves. We will delve into various topics, such as self-esteem, relationships, communication skills, boundaries, and much more.

Through a combination of insightful advice, engaging stories, and fun activities, we hope to inspire and motivate young girls to achieve their full potential.

So whether you are a teenage girl struggling to find your place in the world, a young girl trying to make sense of your changing body, or a parent looking to support your daughter in the best possible way, this book is for you.

Together, we will explore the complexities of growing up and provide you with the tools you need to navigate the journey with confidence and grace. Are you ready? Let's begin!

CHAPTER ONE

Your Guide to Puberty

A person's life undergoes a lot of change during puberty, which may be both thrilling and intimidating. We will talk about the physical changes that take place during puberty in this chapter.

We'll cover everything, from the development of breasts and the start of menstruation to the growth of hair in new locations.

First and foremost, it's critical to comprehend that everyone experiences puberty as a natural process.

During this period, your body begins to develop and you start to transform into an adult.

Hormones, which are chemical messengers made by your body's glands, are what cause the changes that take place during puberty.

The first alteration that happens throughout puberty is the development of new hair.

Boys may notice hair growth on their face, chest, and genitals, while girls frequently experience pubic and underarm hair growth.

Although it may be exciting to see these changes, it's vital to realize that it's also common to feel uncomfortable or self-conscious.

Girls will normally start to develop breasts as puberty progresses. Up until the age of 18, breast growth can begin as early as eight years old.

It's critical to realize that every girl's breasts will develop uniquely and that breast development is a gradual process.

It's very common for some ladies to feel painful or sore in their breasts during this time.

The start of menstruation is a significant shift that happens during puberty.

Menstruation is a normal bodily function that takes place when the uterine lining sheds and blood leaks from the vagina.

The average age at which menstruation begins is 12, however it can happen at any age between 8 and 16 years old.

It's critical that females comprehend that menstruation is a natural occurrence and that there is no reason to feel ashamed about it.

Emotional changes also take place during puberty in addition to physical ones. Teenagers frequently experience mood fluctuations brought on by hormones, including emotions of melancholy, worry, or impatience.

It's critical to keep in mind that these emotional shifts are a typical aspect of puberty and will eventually pass.

It's also critical to realize that everyone goes through puberty in their own unique way. Some individuals may experience puberty sooner or later than their classmates, and some individuals may go through more profound changes.

It's crucial to keep in mind that everyone develops at their own rate and to refrain from comparing yourself to others.

Puberty is a period of profound physical and emotional transformation.

Hormones are the primary cause of the physical changes that occur during puberty, and each person has a unique experience.

It's critical to realize that these changes are common and nothing to be embarrassed about. Never be reluctant to speak with a trustworthy adult or healthcare professional if you have any queries or worries about puberty.

They can offer you the advice and assistance you require during this thrilling and perhaps difficult period.

The Timeline of Puberty

Due to the fact that it signifies the passage from childhood to adolescent, puberty is a key turning point in a person's life. Physical, mental, and social changes are occurring throughout this time, which can be both thrilling and difficult at times.

Therefore, it's critical to have a thorough awareness of what to anticipate throughout this time. Understanding the chronology of puberty is one approach to do this.

Between the ages of 8 and 13 for girls and 9 to 14 for boys, puberty normally starts.

Puberty might begin earlier or later than this typical schedule, but it's important to remember that everyone is unique. From two to five years can pass throughout the puberty phase.

The appearance of breast buds is typically the earliest indication of puberty in girls.

It may occur as young as age 8 or as old as age 13. Increased estrogen production results in the growth of breast tissue, which leads to breast development.

Girls have pubic hair growth during breast development, which is followed by the start of menstruation, which normally happens around age 12 or 13.

Around age 11 or 12, boys typically experience testicular growth, which is the earliest sign of puberty. A few months later, pubic hair growth begins as a result.

Boys will have penile growth following pubic hair growth, and eventually develop face and body hair.

When a person reaches puberty, their voice deepens significantly. This normally happens between the ages of 12 and 16.

The growth spurt is a substantial shift that occurs throughout puberty in both boys and girls. Boys and girls often experience this around the ages of 11 and 13.

Both height and weight are rapidly increasing throughout this time. For girls, this growth spurt can last up to two years, whereas for boys it can extend up to four years.

Puberty can cause emotional and social changes in addition to physical ones.

Teenagers may go through emotional swings, develop more sensitivity, and change how they interact with their family and friends.

It's critical to keep in mind that these changes are common during puberty and occur in everyone.

For teenagers to comprehend the changes they will go through during puberty, the puberty timeline is a crucial resource.

Even while each person's experience with puberty may be a little different, knowing the timeline might make teenagers feel more ready for what's to come.

Understanding the puberty timeline can assist parents, caregivers, and educators support and mentor teenagers during this crucial stage in their life.

Why the Emotions?

Teenage girls experience a wide range of emotions as they navigate through puberty and adolescence. Some common emotions that teenage girls may experience include:

Happiness: Teenage girls may feel happy and joyful when they achieve something, receive praise, or spend time with friends and family.

Sadness: Sadness is a normal part of life, but it can be more intense during adolescence due to hormonal changes and social pressures. Teenage girls may feel sad or down when they experience a loss, breakup, or other difficult situation.

Anger: Anger is a natural emotion that can be triggered by frustration, disappointment, or injustice. Teenage girls may become angry with their parents, peers, or authority figures when they feel misunderstood or treated unfairly.

Fear: Fear is a common emotion during adolescence as teenage girls face new challenges and uncertainties. They may be afraid of failure, rejection, or the unknown.

Anxiety: Anxiety is a feeling of worry or unease that can be persistent and overwhelming. Teenage girls may experience anxiety about school, relationships, or their future.

Excitement: Teenage girls may feel excited when they try new things, meet new people, or anticipate an upcoming event or opportunity.

Love: Romantic love is a common emotion during adolescence as teenage girls develop crushes and relationships. They may also feel love and affection for their family and friends.

Jealousy: Jealousy can arise when teenage girls feel threatened by others' success, popularity, or relationships. They may feel envious or resentful and may struggle with self-esteem and confidence.

You go through a variety of feelings that are common to growing up. It's crucial that you develop good coping mechanisms for managing your emotions and, when necessary, ask for help from responsible adults.

You can go through a lot of emotions, change, and growth at this time. Teenage females frequently experience sudden highs and lows that make them feel as though they are on an emotional rollercoaster.

Let's examine some of the most typical feelings experienced by teenage girls in more detail and then explore what those feelings might actually be like.

The first is fear. We've all experienced it, that sensation of anxiety or stress that can keep us awake at night. Teenage females may experience anxiety due to a variety of circumstances, including impending exams, awkward social settings, or personal issues.

Imagine yourself as a teenage girl who is about to take a significant exam in your least favored subject. You start to feel more and more apprehensive as the day draws closer. You can have physical tension, a pounding heart, and dry skin.

It's possible that you'll find it difficult to focus or that you won't be able to breathe.

Although dealing with anxiety might be difficult, there are methods that can be used, such as talking to a trusted adult or friend, or using relaxation techniques like deep breathing or meditation.

Excitement: Excitation is the antithesis of anxiety. Teenage females are exuberant and enthusiastic, and they frequently want to try new things and take chances.

When was the last time you were genuinely enthusiastic about something? Perhaps it was when you learned your favorite band was playing in town or when you learned you had been accepted to your dream school.

A road trip with friends, a new pastime, or even just thinking about the future can all be exciting activities for teenage ladies.

You might experience an adrenaline rush, a rise in heart rate, and a feeling of anticipation when you're excited. It's a wonderful feeling that can motivate you to pursue your goals and ambitions.

Sadness: Regrettably, not all feelings are good ones. Teenage girls can experience sadness, loneliness, and despair just like everyone else.

Numerous events, such as a breakup, a family crisis, or simply feeling cut off from the outside world, might cause these emotions.

Being sad can be a difficult emotion to handle, so it's crucial to keep in mind that asking for assistance is perfectly acceptable.

Speak to a friend or member of your family, or think about seeing a therapist or counselor. You don't have to experience sadness alone; remember that it's common to feel depressed occasionally.

A legendary teenage temper tantrum comes to me when I think of anger. Teenagers are known for being prone to irrational outrage, whether it is about trivial things like a filthy room or major things like arguments with friends.

It's critical to discover appropriate ways to express the strong feeling of anger because it may be quite destructive.

Imagine yourself as a teenage girl debating with your best friend about an incident that occurred at school. You can feel your blood starting to boil as the dispute becomes more heated.

Even if you might want to scream or hurl something, you take a deep breath and calmly convey your position. Although it's challenging, developing effective anger management skills will benefit you throughout your life.

These are just a handful of the diverse emotions that adolescent females experience on a regular basis. It's important to keep in mind that emotions are a normal and natural component of being a human, therefore you should feel whatever you're feeling.

Don't be hesitant to ask for assistance if you're having emotional difficulties. No matter what, there are those who care about you and want to stand by you.

OH no! What's this on My Chest

Girls' breasts begin to develop between the ages of 8 and 13; it may take several years for them to fully develop. What causes this to occur?

The body begins manufacturing the hormones that are in charge of these changes during puberty. Breast tissue specifically grows as a result of estrogen.

I'm aware of your thoughts at this point. Why must I put up with this uncomfortable situation?

Why can't I just move on and bypass this part? Unfortunately, that's not how our bodies operate. The good news is that everyone else is experiencing the same thing!

What breast changes might you anticipate experiencing as you enter puberty?

You might initially detect a few little lumps or bumps under your nipples.

This simply indicates that your breast buds are beginning to form, which is completely normal.

Your nipples and areolas may also grow larger and darker in color as your breasts continue to expand and round out.

Additionally, it's crucial to recognize that each girl's experience with breast development is different. Some people might begin or finish later than others, and some people might grow more than others.

It's all a part of life's lovely variety!

But let's return for a second to the humor. Ever hear the proverb, "Bras are like friends, close to your heart and there for support"?

That remark, unfortunately, becomes all too true during puberty. You might discover that you need to start wearing a bra for support and comfort as your breasts change and develop.

And believe me when I say that selecting the ideal bra may be a trip in and of itself. However, there are many choices available, and locating the best one for you may be an enjoyable trip.

So, you notice something strange on your chest when you wake up one day. What is that bump? Is it an insect bite? Not at all, it's a breast! You've just started your puberty, congratulations!

When you first start noticing changes in your body, it's perfectly normal to feel a little perplexed or even freaked out.

But rest assured—it's all a necessary aspect of development. In fact, one of the earliest indications that a girl is starting puberty is the development of her breasts.

You might notice some changes in the way your breasts feel and look as they begin to develop.

Even if you observe that one breast is developing more quickly than the other, this is also entirely normal.

There is no "right" or "wrong" method for breasts to develop; rather, each girl's body develops at her own rate.

During this time, some girls may also suffer sensitivity or pain in their breasts.

This is because, if you decide to breastfeed later in age, the breast tissue is developing and expanding to make space for milk ducts, which will eventually produce milk.

Never compare yourself to others; everyone is special in their own way.

Remember that it's acceptable to feel self-conscious about your growing breasts if you do.

Talking to a trustworthy adult, such as your mother or a doctor, can be beneficial if you have any questions or worries.

They can offer you support and make it easier for you to comprehend how your body is changing.

So, accept those developing pains and keep in mind that your changing body is a sign that you're growing into a confident and strong woman!

While often embarrassing and uncomfortable, breast development is a fully natural phase of adolescence.

So accept your body and all of its changes while keeping in mind that everyone else is experiencing the same thing.

Think of bras as your dependable companion who will be by your side through it all if you ever need a laugh.

Facts You Should Know

One of a woman's body's most prominent characteristics are her breasts. They perform a variety of crucial tasks, including feeding infants with milk and enhancing a woman's feeling of femininity.

They are susceptible to a number of health issues, though. We will cover some crucial breast health information and prevention techniques in this chapter.

It's crucial to comprehend the breast's structure first. The breast is composed of fatty tissue, which gives shape and support, and glandular tissue, which produces milk.

The glandular tissue is arranged into lobes, each of which is further subdivided into lobules, or smaller structures.

The lobules generate milk, which is then transferred to the nipple through ducts. The areola, a ring of pigmented skin, encircles the nipple.

Puberty, which can begin as early as eight years old or as late as 14 years old, is when breast development normally starts.

The body begins to create more estrogen during puberty, which causes the development of breast tissue.

Girls and women can have quite different breast sizes and shapes, and these characteristics can alter over the course of a woman's life as a result of conditions like weight increase or loss, pregnancy, and menopause.

One of the most prevalent health issues involving the breasts is breast cancer. Men can develop breast cancer, but women are significantly more likely to do so.

In actuality, one in eight women is predicted to experience breast cancer at some point in their life.

Early detection is crucial for effective treatment, thus it's crucial to undertake routine breast self-exams and to follow your doctor's advice about clinical breast exams and mammograms.

Other medical conditions can also have an impact on the breasts, in addition to breast cancer. For instance, when germs penetrate the breast tissue through a broken or painful nipple, breast infections (mastitis) may result. Antibiotics may be needed to treat these infections, which can result in pain, redness, and swelling in the breast.

A Healthy Breast
There are numerous strategies to maintain healthy breasts.

Wear a bra with support: A supportive bra helps lessen discomfort while exercising and minimize breast drooping.

Maintaining good hygiene: Infections and inflammation can be avoided by keeping the breast area dry and clean.

Regular exercise: Maintaining a healthy weight helps lower the risk of breast-related health issues. Exercise can help with this.

Maintain a healthy diet: Breast health can be preserved with a balanced diet high in fruits, vegetables, and lean proteins.

Limit alcohol consumption: According to studies, drinking too much alcohol can make you more likely to develop breast cancer.

Get enough sleep: Sleep is important for maintaining a strong immune system and lowering stress, both of which have an effect on breast health.

Conduct routine self-examinations: Teenage females can conduct self-examinations to track changes in their breast tissue and notify their doctor of any anomalies.

Get regular checkups: In order to monitor breast health and identify any possible abnormalities early on, teenage girls should get regular checkups from their doctor.

Remember, always adhere to the above information to keep not just breast but your body!.

It's Red, its My Period!
Congratulations! Your body is changing significantly as a result of your maturation.

As a female, you'll undergo many changes, but getting your period is one of the biggest. It's very acceptable to have concerns and some anxiety around this accomplishment.

But don't worry, this guide has you covered.

Let's define a period first before we move on. Your menstruation, which normally lasts 3 to 7 days, is the loss of the lining of your uterus. Although it often begins around 12 or 13, some females may experience it earlier or later.

Let's now discuss the many phases you will experience as you approach your period.

Stage 1: Puberty Begins The onset of puberty is the first stage towards getting your period.

During this stage, your body will start producing hormones that will lead to the development of secondary sex characteristics like breast development and pubic hair growth. This stage usually starts between the ages of 8 to 13, but it can happen earlier or later for some girls.

Stage 2: Thelarche is a fancy word for breast development. It is the first physical sign that your body is preparing for your period. Breast development usually starts around age 10, but it can happen as early as 8 or as late as 13.

Stage 3: Pubic Hair Growth Pubic hair growth is another sign that your body is preparing for your period. This stage usually starts around the age of 11, but it can happen earlier or later for some girls.

Stage 4: Menarche Menarche is the medical term for your first period. This is a significant milestone, and it usually happens around the age of 12 or 13. However, as we mentioned earlier, it can happen earlier or later for some girls.

Stage 5: Regular Menstrual Cycles Once you've had your first period, you'll enter into a phase where you start having regular menstrual cycles.

This implies that your period will occur roughly once every month. Although every girl's menstrual cycle is different, the typical duration is 28 days.

Let's discuss some frequent queries and worries now that you are aware of the many phases leading up to your period.

Q: What is PMS?

A: PMS stands for Pre-Menstrual Syndrome. It refers to the emotional and physical symptoms that some girls experience in the days leading up to their period.

Symptoms can include cramps, mood swings, bloating, and acne. If you experience PMS, talk to your doctor about ways to manage your symptoms.

Q: How do I know when my period is coming?

A: There are a few signs that your period is on the way. You may experience cramping, bloating, and breast tenderness.

You may also notice some discharge, which is a thick, white, or clear fluid that comes out of your vagina. It's a good idea to keep track of your menstrual cycle by using a period tracking app or calendar.

Q: What do I do if I get my period at school?

A: Don't panic! It's perfectly normal to feel a little embarrassed or anxious about getting your period at school, but remember that it's a natural process.

In most schools, the nurse's office or restroom are stocked with supplies like pads and tampons. A spare pad or tampon should always be kept in your bag or backpack just in case.

It's common and natural to have your period as you grow older.

As you approach your first period, there are a few more crucial things to keep in mind in addition to taking good care of your body by eating a healthy diet, getting enough sleep, and exercising. Investigate them below:

Eating a Balanced Diet: Eating a balanced diet is crucial for maintaining overall health, including reproductive health.

Healthy menstrual cycles can be supported by eating a diet high in fruits, vegetables, lean protein, and whole grains.

Additionally, you should try to stay away from processed meals, sugary beverages, and too much caffeine because these can all be detrimental to your menstrual health.

Managing Stress: Stress can have a significant impact on your menstrual cycle. When you're stressed, your body produces higher levels of the hormone cortisol, which can disrupt your menstrual cycle.

It's important to find healthy ways to manage stress, such as practicing relaxation techniques like yoga or deep breathing, spending time with friends and family, or engaging in a hobby you enjoy.

Maintaining Good Hygiene: As you approach your first period, it's important to start practicing good hygiene habits to keep your genital area clean and healthy.

You should aim to wash your genital area with mild soap and water daily, and change your underwear and menstrual products regularly to prevent the buildup of bacteria.

Understanding Your Body: As you progress towards your first period, it's important to start paying attention to your body's natural signs and signals.

You may notice changes in vaginal discharge, breast tenderness, or mood swings as your body prepares for menstruation.

Understanding these changes and talking to a trusted adult or healthcare provider can help you feel more prepared and confident as you approach your first period.

Having Access to Menstrual Products: Once you start your It's crucial to have access to menstrual supplies like pads, tampons, or menstrual cups during your period.

To avoid leaks or infections, you need also be aware of how to use them correctly and how frequently to change them. If you have queries or worries concerning menstruation products, consult a trusted adult or a healthcare professional.

You can encourage healthy menstrual cycles by concentrating on these important areas, and you'll feel more ready when your first period approaches.

It's important to keep in mind that menstruation is a normal aspect of the growth of women and is not something to be ashamed of.

You may feel confident and in control as you traverse adolescence and beyond by taking care of your body and being aware of your needs.

Oh, proper hygiene! For teenage females who are developing and going through their first period, it's not just important to smell nice and clean.

Let's start by discussing the significance of excellent hygiene during puberty. When a girl begins her period, significant changes occur in her body.

During the two to seven days that her menstrual flow lasts, her body is releasing blood and other components. If not handled appropriately, this may result in certain odors and bacterial accumulation.

Now picture yourself as a teenage girl who is beginning to observe physical changes in her body.

Your period is coming every month, and you're growing hair in places you never imagined you would. Although it may feel daunting, excellent hygiene may really make a difference.

What can you do to stay clean at this period, then? Let's begin with the fundamentals.

Daily bathing or showering is necessary. Make sure to wash your entire body, including your private parts, with soap. By doing this, you can fight off bacteria and stay healthy all day.

Regularly replacing your sanitary items is a crucial component of maintaining optimum cleanliness throughout your period.

Depending on your flow, this can entail replacing your pad, tampon, or menstrual cup every 3-6 hours. It's crucial to keep an eye on this because you don't want to risk leaks or odors.

Make careful to select the appropriate pads and tampons for you while we're talking about them. Girls tend to use pads, tampons, or menstrual cups differently.

There are several variations available, so test a few and find one suits your physique the best.

Let's discuss about how important it is to dress cleanly to finish. Your sweat glands are working overtime during puberty, making it simple for scents to accumulate on your clothing.

It's important to remember to change your clothes every day, especially your underwear.

Consider wearing breathable materials as well, such as cotton, to keep you feeling light and airy.

Remember, maintaining excellent hygiene doesn't have to be difficult during puberty. You can feel assured and energetic all day long if you only take care of yourself.

How Will I Know?
The first period!!!

It's a milestone in every young girl's life.

But how will you know when it's happening?

Will there be a sign?

A clue?

A warning?

Young Padawan, do not be afraid; I am here to help you navigate this significant occasion.

Let's start by discussing what a period is in actuality. It is the shedding of the uterine lining, which happens to fertile women each month.

It's an indication that your body is getting ready for a potential pregnancy. The body sheds the lining if the egg that is produced during ovulation is not fertilized since then it no longer needs it.

So how will you be able to predict the arrival of your first period? There are a few warning indicators:

Discharge: About 6 months to a year before your first period, you may start to notice a white or yellowish discharge in your underwear. This is completely normal and is a sign that your body is preparing for menstruation.

Cramps: Some girls experience mild cramps in their lower abdomen or back a few days before their period starts. This is also normal and nothing to worry about.

Mood swings: Hormonal changes can cause mood swings, so if you're feeling a bit more emotional than usual, it could be a sign that your first period is on its way.

Breast tenderness: Just like with PMS, your breasts may feel sore or tender before your period starts.

Spotting: Sometimes, girls experience light spotting or staining in their underwear before their first period. This is also normal and nothing to worry about.

Now, if you do get your period, don't panic! It's a natural and normal part of growing up. Here are a few things to keep in mind:

Use sanitary products: There are lots of options when it comes to menstrual products, including pads, tampons, and menstrual cups. Try a few different options to see what works best for you.

Keep track of your cycle: It's a good idea to keep a calendar or use an app to track when your period starts and ends. This can help you anticipate when it's coming and prepare accordingly.

Don't be afraid to talk to someone: Ask your mother, older sister, or a trustworthy instructor for help if you have any questions or concerns about your period. It's fine to have questions, and it's crucial to feel at ease discussing your body.

Take care of yourself: As we've already covered, it's important to take care of yourself during puberty. A healthy diet, appropriate sleep, and regular exercise should all be priorities.

Remember that while getting your first period is significant, you shouldn't feel embarrassed about it.

It's an indication that your body is functioning as it should and a sign that you're maturing.

Accept it, and don't be hesitant to ask for assistance or suggestions when you require it..

Hey, do this and not this!

During your period, there are certain foods and activities that you may want to avoid or limit to help ease your symptoms. Here are some things to consider:

Processed Foods: It's best to avoid processed foods during your period as they can exacerbate inflammation, bloating, and cramping.

These foods include fried foods, sugary snacks, and packaged snacks.

Caffeine: Caffeine is a stimulant that can increase tension and anxiety, making menstrual cramps worse. So it's best to avoid or limit caffeine intake during your period.

Alcohol: Drinking alcohol during your period can make cramps and bloating worse. Plus, it can also cause dehydration, which can worsen headaches and fatigue.

Salt: Sodium can cause bloating and water retention, so it's best to limit your intake of salty foods during your period.

Strenuous exercise: While it's important to stay active during your period, high-intensity or strenuous exercise can actually increase cramping and discomfort. Instead, try low-impact exercises like yoga, Pilates, or walking.

Tight Clothing: Wearing tight clothing like skinny jeans, tight skirts, or leggings can constrict your blood flow and cause discomfort. Opt for looser, more comfortable clothing during your period.

Smoking: Smoking could worsen cramps and raise the possibility of menstruation difficulties. The best course of action is to completely stop smoking, especially while on your period.

There are some things you might want to avoid doing or eating during your period to make things a little easier on yourself, even though it's a completely normal and natural part of life.

Let's start by talking about food. While a family-sized bag of potato chips or a pint of ice cream may be alluring to you during your period, you may want to reconsider indulging in excessive amounts of salty or sweet treats.

Nobody wants their bloating or cramps to get worse because of this. Instead, make an effort to increase your intake of fruits, veggies, and whole grains to help maintain your body in balance.

Let's now discuss activities. Even while it's crucial to maintain a healthy lifestyle during your period, there are some items you may wish to avoid.

For instance, strenuous exercise or activities that require a lot of leaping or bouncing may be uncomfortable or even painful for a woman during her period.

So perhaps forgo the trampoline park for a few days and substitute yoga or a brisk stroll for something more low-impact.

Additionally, it's generally advisable to avoid swimming in pools or other bodies of water while on your period unless you're using a menstrual cup or tampon.

In addition to being painful, it may also expose others to bacteria or other germs.

Finally, despite the fact that we all adore coffee, it's better to avoid it during your period. Caffeine can increase your anxiety and jitteriness and perhaps make cramps and bloating worse.

Ladies, that's all there is to it! Several things to bear in mind during your period. It all comes down to self-care and paying attention to your body. Additionally, there is always chocolate available!

But It's Painful!

The delights of puberty, ah! In addition to the physical changes, dealing with PMS (premenstrual syndrome) and the delightful cramps that accompany it may be an emotional rollercoaster. But do not worry, dear readers; in this chapter, we will cover all the information you require regarding PMS and cramps.

Let's define PMS first things first. Many girls and women suffer premenstrual syndrome, a collection of physical and mental symptoms, before to their period.

Bloating, mood changes, headaches, and acne are a few examples of these symptoms. PMS can endure from a few days to a week and usually starts the week before a girl's period.

Let's now discuss those cramps. Cramps, a typical menstrual symptom, can range in intensity from mild discomfort to incapacitating pain.

In order to lose its lining, which is important for the monthly flow, the uterus contracts, which is what causes them. The lower belly, lower back, and perhaps even the thighs may experience pain and discomfort during these contractions.

What then can you do to lessen the suffering that comes with PMS and cramps?

Here are a few tips:

Exercise - Believe it or not, exercise can actually help alleviate the symptoms of PMS and cramps.

It helps to release endorphins, which are natural painkillers, and can also reduce bloating and boost your mood.

So go ahead and hit the gym, take a yoga class, or go for a walk - your body will thank you.

Heat - Applying heat to your lower abdomen can help to relax the muscles and ease the pain of cramps. You can use a heating pad, a hot water bottle, or even take a warm bath.

Pain relievers - Over-the-counter pain relievers such as ibuprofen or naproxen can help to reduce the pain and discomfort of cramps.

Just be sure to follow the dosage instructions and consult with your doctor if you have any concerns.

Good nutrition - Eating a healthy, balanced diet can help to reduce PMS symptoms and provide your body with the nutrients it needs to function properly.

Be sure to include plenty of fruits and vegetables, whole grains, and lean proteins in your diet.

Rest - Getting enough sleep and rest is important for overall health, but it's especially important during PMS and menstruation. Make sure to prioritize rest and relaxation during this time and listen to your body when it needs a break.

And now, for a little comic relief - here are a few things NOT to do during PMS and menstruation:

Do NOT watch sad movies or listen to sad music unless you want to end up crying for hours on end.

Do NOT wear your favorite white pants unless you want to risk staining them.

Do NOT go swimming unless you have a tampon or menstrual cup - trust us on this one.

Do NOT forget to pack extra pads or tampons when you're on the go - you never know when you might need them.

And finally, don't listen to others who tell you that you're "overreacting" or that you're being "too emotional" because PMS and menstruation are very real, and it's crucial to take care of yourself during this time.

Consider yourself at a fair and you come across two rides, one of which is called "PMS" and the other is called "Cramps."

Both the PMS ride and the Cramps ride include signs that read, "Twists and Turns, Guaranteed to Make You Squirm!" and "Mood Swings Galore!" respectively.

You choose to ride the PMS ride first and notice that you are starting to feel a little irritable as soon as you step on.

The journey abruptly changes course, leaving you feeling irritated, angry, and depressed all at once.

When you're about to lose it, the ride changes directions, and before you know it, you're giggling uncontrollably.

You choose to ride the Cramps ride after exiting the PMS ride. Your stomach begins to ache slowly as soon as you sit down.

The aching develops into a severe pain as the ride begins to spin and twist. Although you make an effort to cling on, the anguish just gets worse.

The ride finally comes to an end, and you stagger away feeling worn out and aching.

However, unlike a carnival ride, PMS and cramps are not genuinely enjoyable.

You now know everything there is to know about PMS and cramps, folks. Every girl's experience is unique, so pay attention to your body and do what feels right to you.

Above all, remember to be nice and compassionate to yourself because puberty can be tough, but so are you!

Tampons vs Pads

The monthly onset of your period is just one of the numerous things you'll experience at this time.

Although it can be overwhelming and perplexing, don't worry; we're here to explain the distinctions between pads and tampons.

Let's start by talking about pads. Pads come in a variety of sizes and forms to suit your needs and are worn outside of the body in your underwear.

They contain an adhesive strip that clings to your underwear to keep them in place and are constructed of absorbent materials to soak up menstrual flow.

Pads are simple to use and ideal for people who are new to menstruation or who would rather not have anything inserted into their body.

Tampons, on the other hand, are placed inside the vagina and are made of materials that absorbingly expand to gather menstrual flow.

They also feature a string that hangs outside of your body for simple removal and available in various sizes and forms to suit your needs.

Tampons are ideal for people who want to be more active during their period and don't want to worry about a bulky pad, such as swimming or playing sports.

After covering the essentials, let's move on to some funny contrasts between pads and tampons.

If you're concerned about leaks, pads are like a safety net for your period since they collect everything that comes out. Contrarily, tampons act as a small army of soldiers that enter your vagina to take care of business.

Pads can be embarrassing since they generate an audible "fwap fwap" sound while you walk. Although tampons are silent, you might be concerned about leaving the string from your bikini bottoms at the beach by accident.

Pads might make you feel like a baby because they are similar to wearing diapers. The difference between tampons and a ninja in your vagina is that you can't even tell they're there!

Let's discuss some important factors to take into account while deciding between pads and tampons.

When worn for an extended period of time, pads can chafe and feel thick and uncomfortable.

Tampons can raise the risk of toxic shock syndrome, an uncommon but dangerous bacterial infection, if they are not changed frequently enough.

It's critical to pick a menstruation product that gives you confidence and comfort during your period.

So that you may locate the product that works for you, don't be afraid to explore and test out several options.

It's important to acknowledge your period and appreciate your body, whether you decide to use pads or tampons.

Your period is only one aspect of the fascinating journey that is puberty. You can navigate through this experience with confidence and easily if you have the necessary information and mindset.

A Quick Review of What's Normal (And What's Not)

Puberty can be a confusing and challenging time, and it's normal to have questions about what's happening to your body.

But how do you know what's normal and what's not? In this chapter, we'll review some of the most common changes that happen during puberty and help you understand what to expect.

Breast Development: It's normal for one breast to grow faster or be larger than the other.

Breast tissue can also feel lumpy or tender, especially right before your period.

However, if you notice a lump that feels hard, doesn't move around easily, or is accompanied by discharge or pain, it's important to see a doctor.

Body Hair: As your hormones change, you may notice more hair growing in new places, such as your underarms, legs, and pubic area.

This is normal, but if you notice excessive hair growth or hair in unexpected places, it may be a sign of a hormonal imbalance and you should talk to your doctor.

Menstruation: The menstrual cycle can vary from person to person, but on average, it lasts about 28 days.

While some cramps and discomfort are common during your period, it's vital to see your doctor if you feel extreme pain, excessive bleeding, or periods that last longer than a week.

Acne: Hormonal changes associated with puberty can increase oil production, which results in acne.

It's natural to have some pimples or blemishes, but it's crucial to contact a dermatologist if you have severe acne or scarring.

Mood Swings: Hormonal changes can also affect your emotions, leading to mood swings, irritability, and anxiety.

It's important to take care of your mental health during this time and seek help if you feel overwhelmed or depressed.

It's typical to go through a variety of physical and emotional changes during puberty because it's a time of growth and change.

However, don't be afraid to speak with a trusted adult or healthcare professional if you observe any changes that appear unexpected or troubling.

There is no one "right" way to experience puberty because each person's body is different and individual.

A Trip to the Gynecologist

Ah, the gynecologist, a doctor that most young girls would want to avoid but ultimately must see. Although it can be frightening, the experience is crucial.

So let's discuss what to anticipate and how to get ready for your first appointment to the gynecologist.

Let's start by asking why you need to see a gynecologist. They are experts in the female reproductive system, to start.

It's crucial to have a specialist who can address your questions and concerns while also assisting you in maintaining your health.

What takes place during the initial visit, then?

It's not as scary as it seems, so don't worry. The doctor or nurse practitioner will first ask you about your medical background, including any previous operations, drugs, allergies, and diseases.

Inquiries concerning your menstrual cycle, sexual behavior, and use of contraceptives will also be made.

The medical professional will then conduct a physical examination. This will involve a pelvic check as well as a breast exam.

The doctor will look for any lumps or abnormalities during the breast exam.

During the pelvic exam, the vagina, cervix, and uterus are examined for any indications of infection, unusual growths, or other problems.

Although it could be uncomfortable, it shouldn't hurt. Do not be afraid to speak out and let the doctor know if you are uneasy.

Let's now discuss how to get ready for the visit.

Plan the appointment for a time when you are not in menstruation.

Avoid using any vaginal products, such as creams or douches, for at least 24 hours prior to the exam, and dress comfortably in loose-fitting clothing. Bringing a list of potential questions for the doctor is also a good idea.

Remember that your gynecologist is there to assist you, so don't be shy about raising any issues or questions you may have.

So that you feel comfortable speaking with your gynecologist in the future, it's critical to build a strong rapport with them as soon as possible.

Although going to the gynecologist for the first time can be intimidating, doing so is an important first step in maintaining your reproductive health.

Prepare yourself, ask questions, and don't be hesitant to speak out if something makes you feel uneasy. And constantly keep in mind that you are not alone. The same thing has happened to millions of other girls, and they all survived.

CHAPTER TWO

Bit by Bit, Your Body is growing

Starting at the Top: The Hair on Your Head

Hello, gorgeous locks! You will start to notice changes in your hair as you get older.

That can entail coping with oily hair or dandruff for some people while thicker, fuller locks for others. However, there's no need to worry because we've got you covered for anything hair-related.

Let's start by discussing the science of hair growth. On your scalp, each hair follicle has a cycle of growth, rest, and shedding.

Each cycle's duration and the rate of growth can differ from person to person. You may notice changes in the texture or thickness of your hair during puberty since hormones can also impact the development cycle of your hair.

Let's now delve into the specifics of hair care. First things first, cleaning your hair is necessary, but doing so too frequently might be detrimental.

You might be tempted to wash your hair every day if you have oily hair because doing so might rob it of its natural oils and leave it dry and brittle.

On the other side, you might not need to wash your hair as frequently if it is dry. How frequently should you wash your hair, then?

Your own preferences and the type of hair you have actually determine this. Some people can go a week without washing their hair, while others wash it every other day.

There are so many alternatives available when picking a shampoo and conditioner that it can be confusing.

The good news is that you don't have to spend a fortune on a quality item. It's vital to use conditioner as well since it can help nourish your hair and avoid tangles.

Look for a shampoo that is gentle and devoid of sulfates because they can be harsh on your hair. Make sure to completely clean it to prevent any buildup.

It might be enjoyable to express yourself through your hairstyle, but it's crucial to treat it gently.

Breakage and damage to your hair might result from pulling it back too tightly or using heat styling equipment too frequently.

Use a heat protectant spray and keep the temperature moderate if you do use heat styling tools.

Let's discuss about hair removal last but not least. It's normal to develop pubic hair as you get older, and there is nothing wrong with it.

If you decide to have your pubic hair removed, make sure to do so responsibly.

Waxing can be uncomfortable and expensive, while shaving can cause discomfort and ingrown hairs. Think about other choices like hair removal treatments or clipping.

You now know everything there is to know about hair care. Keep in mind that each person has unique hair, so what works for your friend might not work for you.

Try out several products and methods until you discover the one that best suits you and your gorgeous locks!

My Ears are so Dear

Although they might not look like the most interesting portion of your body, they are quite crucial!

You can hear, balance, and even control your body temperature with the aid of your ears. So let's pay them the respect they merit and educate ourselves on how to properly care for them.

Let's start by discussing the structure of your ears. The outer ear, middle ear, and inner ear are the three sections of your ear.

You can see your earlobe and ear canal since they are both located in the outer ear.

The three tiny bones that transport sound to the inner ear are located in the middle ear, which is the area behind the eardrum.

The cochlea, an organ with a spiral shape found in the inner ear, transforms sound waves into electrical impulses that your brain can understand.

After learning the fundamentals, let's move on to the fun part: caring for your ears! The following advice can help you maintain healthy and happy ears:

Keep your ears clean: It's important to clean your outer ear gently with a washcloth, but never use a cotton swab or any other object that can push earwax further into your ear canal.

This can cause irritation, infection, and even damage to your eardrum.

Protect your ears: Loud noises can damage your ears over time, so it's important to protect them when you're around loud sounds.

Wear earplugs or earmuffs when you're at concerts, sporting events, or other noisy environments.

Don't stick anything in your ear: We know we just said this, but it's worth repeating. Never put anything smaller than your elbow in your ear! That means no cotton swabs, pencils, or anything else that could damage your ear canal or eardrum.

Check for signs of infection: If you notice any pain, swelling, or discharge from your ear, it could be a sign of an infection. Talk to your doctor if you experience any of these symptoms.

Get your ears checked: It's a good idea to have your ears checked by a doctor or audiologist every few years, especially if you've been exposed to loud noises or have a history of ear infections.

Now, let's get a little comical with our ear care advice. Did you know that earwax is actually good for you?

It helps keep your ears lubricated and protects them from bacteria and other harmful substances.

So, don't be too quick to clean out all your earwax - a little bit is actually a good thing!

Another fun fact: Did you realize that your ears' shape might impact how well you hear?

The way that people with large ears and those with small ears perceive sound may differ.

In addition, did you know that some animals, such as dogs and cats, have the ability to hear frequencies that are too high for humans to hear?

Therefore, if your animal friend perk up their ears the next time you see them, they might be hearing something you can't!

In conclusion, paying love and care to your ears is necessary because they are a vital component of your body.

You can keep them healthy and content for years to come by adhering to these suggestions. Let's give our ears a round of applause as they are "ears so dear"!

Eyes That See

Your eyes and all the great things they can do will be the topic of our discussion.

Your eyes are really beautiful. You can see the world around you in all of its exquisite hues and forms because they are the windows to your spirit. However, you might notice certain changes in your vision as you go through puberty.

Let's begin with the fundamentals. You can see with the assistance of the various components that make up your eyes. The cornea is the front of your eye's transparent outer layer.

Your eye's iris, which is colored, aids in regulating how much light enters your eye. The black dot in the middle of your iris, known as the pupil, changes size in response to the amount of light present.

The retina is the back portion of your eye and includes the cells that enable you to see.

The lens is a transparent structure within your eye that aids in focusing light onto your retina.

Some people may experience changes in their vision throughout puberty, such as nearsightedness or farsightedness.

This implies that you can have problems seeing objects up close or in the distance.

Don't be alarmed if you detect changes in your vision; they are quite natural. You might only require contacts or glasses to improve your vision.

However, you can also take care of your eyes in other ways. Most importantly, make sure you get adequate rest!

Aim for 8 to 10 hours of sleep each night since your eyes require rest just as the rest of your body does. When you're outside, you should also wear sunglasses with UV protection to shield your eyes from the sun.

Giving your eyes a vacation from screens is a crucial component of eye care. In the modern world, it's simple to lose hours to a computer or smartphone screen. But doing so can exhaustion and eye strain.

Follow the 20-20-20 rule to avoid this: take a break every 20 minutes and stare at something 20 feet away for 20 seconds. Your eyes will benefit from a break and less strain if you do this.

Last but not least, make sure to schedule routine eye exams with an ophthalmologist or optometrist. They can assess any changes in your eyes and assist you in maintaining good eye health.

No!! You don't understand! Let me explain again!

Did you know that the windows to your soul are your eyes? They may not be exactly your soul, but they are your windows to the outside world!

Amazing little globes called your eyes are what allow you to perceive and appreciate life's beauty.

Let's start off by discussing how crucial your eyes are. Consider all the activities you perform every day with your eyes.

Your eyes are constantly working to assist you in navigating the world around you, whether you're reading, watching TV, catching a ball, or recognizing a friend's face across the room.

But there's more! Your eyes are also highly intricate, with numerous elements that all work together to provide you great vision.

Let's now discuss how gorgeous your eyes are. Did you realize that only you have a set of eyes?

Your eyes have a unique pattern similar to your fingerprints called an iris. They are also gorgeous in other ways.

Have you ever been mesmerized by the color or shine of someone else's eyes?

That's because your eyes are more than just tiny balls; they are also framed by delicate lashes and formed specifically for you by the shape of your bones.

Your eyes are extremely unique and lovely because of how these factors work together.

So, the next time you glance in the mirror, stop to admire those lovely orbs that are reflecting back at you.

And don't forget to look after them as well! Wear sunglasses to shield them from UV rays, and make sure they get enough rest and fluids to stay hydrated and healthy.

In conclusion, your eyes are stunning and magnificent in their current state. So pause for a moment to acknowledge them and all the wonders they make possible.

Therefore, look after those priceless eyes of yours! They will continue to shine brightly with a little care.

Ahhh!! My Face!!

Although it's true that "beauty is only skin deep," taking care of your skin has benefits that go beyond aesthetics.

Your skin, which is the largest organ in your body, protects you from the elements, controls your body's temperature, and even produces vitamin D.

How then do you maintain the health of your skin on your face? Here are some pointers:

Wash your face twice a day: Cleaning your face with soap and water can help get rid of oil, grime, and other pollutants that might clog your pores and cause breakouts.

Avoid rubbing your face too hard and use a light cleanser to prevent irritation.

Moisturize daily: Keeping your skin hydrated is important, even if you have oily skin. Use a lightweight moisturizer that won't clog your pores, and apply it after washing your face.

Wear sunscreen: Protecting your skin from the sun's harmful rays can help prevent premature aging and reduce your risk of skin cancer.

Look for a sunscreen with an SPF of at least 30, and apply it every day, even on cloudy days.

Avoid touching your face: Your hands come into contact with a lot of germs throughout the day, and touching your face can transfer those germs to your skin, leading to breakouts and infections.

Now, let's take a look at some case studies to see how these tips can be put into practice.

Case Study 1: Jane's Story

Jane, a 16-year-old female, has battled acne for many years. Every over-the-counter acne medication she could find has been tried, but nothing has seemed to work. She finally makes the choice to visit a dermatologist.

The doctor suggests a straightforward skincare regimen that includes twice-daily face washing with a mild cleanser, the use of a light moisturizer, and the use of a topical acne treatment.

The dermatologist also recommends that she use sunscreen every day and refrain from touching her face.

Following the dermatologist's recommendations for a few weeks, Jane begins to notice a noticeable improvement in her skin.

Her skin looks healthier and more radiant as her acne clears up.

Case Study 2: Zoe's Story

The 14-year-old girl named Zoe enjoys playing sports outside.

She's frightened that she's getting wrinkles at an early age because she's noticed that her skin has turned dry and flaky.

Her mother advises her to start applying moisturizer daily and to wear sunscreen whenever she is outside. In order to stay hydrated, she also counsels her to drink a lot of water.

Although Zoe's mother explains that there are lightweight moisturizers available that won't clog her pores, Zoe initially objects to using a moisturizer because she fears it will make her skin oily.

Additionally, she assists her in choosing a sunscreen that she enjoys and exhorts her to use it each day.

Following her mother's advice for a few weeks, Zoe has seen a difference in the softness and smoothness of her skin as well as the disappearance of the dryness and flakiness.

She is especially pleased with how much younger and healthier her skin seems.

It may feel like a chore to take care of your face and skin, but it's crucial to keep in mind that healthy skin is beautiful skin.

You can look and feel your best every day by adhering to these easy suggestions and taking the time to care for your skin.

Keep in mind that maintaining your face doesn't have to be difficult or expensive.

Always cleanse your face before bed and wear sunscreen during the day, as your mother said.

In the event that everything else fails, simply don a huge hat and some sunglasses and call it a day. You'll still look gorgeous, we promise.

The No Grief Teeth!

You now have to worry about keeping your teeth clean and healthy on top of dealing with all the changes to your body.

But don't worry—we're here to make it as enjoyable and painless as we can!

Let's start by discussing the fundamentals of oral hygiene.

You undoubtedly already know how vital it is to clean your teeth twice a day, but did you also know how crucial flossing is?

Yes, we are aware that flossing may be a hassle. Let's just say it's not the most enjoyable activity. But have faith—it'll be worthwhile in the end.

In addition to removing food fragments and plaque from between your teeth, flossing also aids in avoiding foul breath and gum disease. Who wants to handle those, though?

Let's now discuss some typical dental issues that can arise during adolescence. Overcrowding is among the most widespread problems.

Sometimes, when your jaw develops and changes shape, this can result in your teeth crowding and being out of alignment.

This might not only change how your smile looks, but it can also make it more difficult to adequately brush and floss your teeth.

The good news is that there are many alternatives, including braces and clear aligners, for correcting crowding.

Wisdom teeth are another frequent problem. Those annoying teeth that always seem to cause issues, ah, sure.

Wisdom teeth often begin to erupt in the late teens or early twenties, and they can result in a variety of issues, including discomfort, swelling, infection, and even harm to nearby teeth.

In order to avoid future issues, it's critical to consult a dentist as soon as you notice any of these symptoms.

But enough about the unpleasant things; let's talk about the enjoyable part—maintaining gleaming, sound, and healthy teeth!

Eating a nutritious, well-balanced diet that is high in vitamins and minerals is one of the greatest methods to do this.

Get plenty of dairy products, leafy greens, and fortified cereals to ensure you are getting enough calcium, which is particularly crucial for strong teeth and bones.

As these meals can erode your tooth enamel and cause cavities, remember to restrict your intake of sugary and acidic foods.

That concludes our brief and painless tutorial on maintaining your teeth while going through puberty.

Just keep in mind that a beautiful grin is one that is healthy, and there is nothing better than showing off your pearly whites with assurance.

Have you heard about the dentist who wed a nail technician? They battled valiantly! Sorry, we couldn't help ourselves.

Oh, before I overlook

Have you ever questioned why your baby's smile is distinct from that of your grandparents'?

That is because people go through various sets of teeth over the course of their lives! So let's trip through our teeth from conception to demise.

Infants are born without teeth, but they soon begin to grow milk teeth, sometimes referred to as primary teeth.

Around six months of age, these teeth typically begin to erupt, and by the time they are three years old, they will have 20 main teeth in all.

These teeth are necessary for speaking, eating food, and the growth of the facial bones and muscles.

Our baby teeth begin to fall out as we get older, creating room for our permanent teeth, also known as adult teeth.

This often begins around the age of six and can last up until the age of twelve.

The molars, which are found towards the back of the mouth, are the first permanent teeth to erupt. The premolars, canines, and incisors come after these teeth.

We will have 32 teeth when we reach adulthood, including four wisdom teeth. Not everyone develops wisdom teeth, which typically erupt between the ages of 17 and 25.

These teeth may need to be removed in some circumstances because the mouths of some people cannot accommodate them without causing pain and discomfort.

Based on the shape and function of our teeth, there are four different sorts.

Incisors, canines, premolars, and molars are the four different types. The front of the mouth contains incisors, which are used to cut and bite food.

The sharp teeth next to the incisors are called canines, and they are used to rip and shred food.

Food is ground and crushed by the premolars, which are situated in between the canines and the molars. Last but not least, molars are the big, flat teeth in the back of the mouth that are used to crush and grind food.

No matter what stage of life we are in, maintaining our teeth is crucial.

Cavities, gum disease, and other dental issues can be avoided with regular brushing, flossing, and dental checkups.

That concludes the journey through our teeth from conception to demise.

Who knew the modifications to our teeth over the course of a lifetime? So, keep in mind your various tooth types the next time you smile and be sure to look after them!

Remember that sharks can lose and develop up to 50,000 teeth throughout their lifetime, so keep in mind that they have an endless supply of teeth!

So let's appreciate the limited number of teeth we have and treat them well.

You and the Dentist

For most people, the notion of seeing the dentist is terrifying. It can be equally terrifying for girls going through puberty, though.

Do I really need to go to the dentist, you might be thinking. "Yes!" is the unmistakable response.

It's important to take care of your teeth, and this is especially true during puberty when your body is undergoing several changes.

Let's begin with the fundamentals. There are several reasons why your teeth are vital.

They support your confidence when you eat, speak, and smile. Humans have four distinct types of teeth, did you know that? That is correct! We have canines, molars, premolars, and incisors.

The pointed teeth in the front of your mouth known as incisors assist you in biting into food. The sharp teeth next to your incisors called canines aid in tearing and shredding food.

Premolars, which are situated in between the canines and the molars, aid in the crushing and grinding of food.

The largest teeth in the back of your mouth, the molars are in charge of fully grinding and chewing your food.

Your body goes through various changes during puberty that may have an impact on your teeth.

For instance, hormones can increase the sensitivity of your gums, making them more prone to bleeding and irritation. If you don't take good care of your teeth, this could result in gum disease.

Brushing your teeth twice a day and flossing on a regular basis are essential for maintaining dental health.

Remember to go to the dentist for a checkup and cleaning at least twice a year.

Don't worry if you're anxious about visiting the dentist. It's not just you. Here are some suggestions for reducing your anxiety:

Invite a friend or member of your family to the appointment.

During the appointment, listen to audiobooks or music.

To relax, engage in deep breathing techniques.

So that you are aware of what to anticipate, ask your dentist to thoroughly describe the operation to you.

Keep in mind that maintaining good oral health is essential to your overall health and wellbeing. Don't allow fear prevent you from receiving the care you require.

And just consider the fact that when your session is over, you'll have a sparkling grin to flaunt to everyone!

Be brave and sit in the dentist's chair. Your teeth will appreciate it.

Although visiting the dentist may not be the most fun thing ever, it is essential to maintaining strong, healthy teeth.

Who knows, you might even like your stay! Your smile will always remain brilliant as long as you remember to brush, floss, and schedule routine dental appointments.

Beyond Braces!

Braces, ah. The dreaded nightmare for some young kids and a rite of passage for many.

Braces, whether you love them or loathe them, are necessary to straighten your teeth and give you a radiant smile. Prepare yourself for the drama of braces by doing so.

Let's start by discussing what braces are in actuality. Orthodontists utilize braces as tools to straighten the jaw and align the bite.

They are made up of wires that are threaded through the brackets, which are fastened to the teeth with a specific glue.

The teeth are then progressively moved into the proper place by gently tightening and adjusting the wires.

Now, braces can be a real pain in the neck. They may leave you with wounds, soreness, or irritation in your mouth. There are, however, techniques to control the discomfort, so don't worry.

For instance, you can cover the brackets with orthodontic wax to stop them from scraping on your cheeks and gums. You can always use pills to aid with the pain if you're really struggling.

However, the effect braces can have on your social life is where the real drama with braces lies. Braces aren't the most fashionable accessory, let's face it.

However, don't let that prevent you from leading a fulfilling life! There are several ways to embrace your individual style while rocking your braces.

You might have personalized brackets to showcase your unique individuality or choose vibrant bands to embellish your braces.

And if somebody attempts to make fun of your braces or tease you about them, just keep in mind that they are only envious of your commitment to good oral hygiene and a radiant smile.

You will also have the final laugh after your braces come removed!

However, the confidence boost that braces may provide is possibly their largest advantage. You're more inclined to flash your smile and feel confident when you're proud of it.

Therefore, if you're feeling a little self-conscious about having braces, simply keep in mind that they're only a short-term nuisance that will have a long-term payoff.

Although wearing braces may seem like a drama-filled nightmare, they are crucial to achieving a beautiful, healthy smile. So get ready for the road ahead, and don't forget to enjoy yourself a little!

The Underarm is not a Dungeon!

Ah, the underarms. For many people, especially during adolescence, they are a constant source of embarrassment and discomfort.

Fear not, though, my dear reader, for we are here to help you navigate the world of underarm care by providing you with advice, tactics, and a healthy dose of comedy.

Let's first discuss the causes of sweating. When we become too heated, our bodies' natural cooling mechanism is sweating.

Although it's a natural and necessary procedure, there may also be some unfavorable consequences, such as body odor and discolored clothing.

The most crucial aspect of underarm care is to keep the region dry and clean.

This entails cleaning frequently with soap and water and controlling sweat and odor with an antiperspirant or deodorant.

You might be wondering, though, what distinguishes deodorant from antiperspirant.

Antiperspirants are made to prevent sweat from evaporating, but deodorants just cover up odor.

Therefore, if you tend to perspire a lot, you might wish to choose an antiperspirant to keep things under check.

Let's now discuss some typical blunders people make when it comes to caring for their underarms. One of the biggest no-nos is shaving immediately before using deodorant or antiperspirant.

This could irritate people and make it harder for the product to function properly.

The optimum time to shave is at night, and the greatest time to use deodorant or antiperspirant is in the morning.

Using too much product is yet another error. Using too much might actually make matters worse by blocking your pores and retaining sweat and odor. A little goes a long way.

There you have it, folks, a crash course in maintaining your underarms. Keep in mind to keep it clean and dry, and don't be afraid to try out several products until you find the one that works best for you.

If all else fails, just proudly show off your sweaty side and wear those pit stains. After all, who doesn't love a little additional character? They also indicate a healthy and active body.

The underarms are a significant body component that regulate body temperature and sweat production.

But if neglected, they can also develop into a haven for bacteria and other microbes, posing a number of health hazards.

Here are some of the risks associated with not keeping the underarms neat:

Body Odor: The underarms are one of the primary areas where the body produces sweat, which can lead to body odor if not properly managed.

Bacteria thrive in warm and moist environments, and if left unchecked, can quickly lead to an unpleasant smell.

Skin Irritation: If the underarms are not regularly cleaned and dried, they can become irritated, resulting in redness, itching, and even painful rashes.

This can be exacerbated by wearing tight clothing that traps moisture against the skin.

Infections: Bacteria flourish in warm, damp settings and can cause a number of illnesses if left unchecked.

For instance, when hair follicles swell up and develop pimples that are painful and filled with pus, a bacterial infection known as foliculitis may develop.

The same goes for intertrigo, a fungus that can develop in warm, wet skin creases like the underarms.

Staining of Clothes: Additionally, sweat can leave stains on clothing, especially around the underarm area.

Sweat and bacteria buildup can result in ugly yellow stains that are challenging to remove if not routinely washed.

For hygienic and medical reasons, it's critical to maintain neat underarms.

Unpleasant odors, skin irritation, infections, and garment discoloration can be avoided with regular washing, the use of antiperspirants and deodorants, and the use of breathable clothing.

OMG! My Hair!

We will discuss hair, a subject to which we can all relate.

Our bodies' basic component, hair, comes in a variety of forms, hues, and textures. Any type of hair, whether it is long, short, curly, straight, thick, or thin, is attractive in its own special manner.

However, why is hair so crucial?

Well, hair has several uses besides just enhancing your appearance.

It can act as a sensory organ, shield against UV rays, insulate the scalp to assist control body temperature. Additionally, it allows you to express yourself and highlight your personality!

Let's now discuss some of the difficulties associated with hair, particularly in terms of hair maintenance.

We can all relate to the hardship of having a poor hair day, but did you know that ignoring your hair might do permanent harm?

Not taking care of your hair can result in a variety of issues, including split ends and hair loss.

Setting up a hair care program is crucial for maintaining healthy, lustrous hair. Regular cleaning, conditioning, and trimming fall under this category.

Additionally, you can avoid breakage and damage by detangling your hair with a comb or hairbrush.

Be kind, though! Brushing too hard might harm the scalp and cause hair loss.

Avoiding heat damage is an important part of hair care. Hair can become dry and brittle with heat styling appliances like flat irons and blow dryers, which can result in breakage and split ends.

Use a heat protectant and only use heated styling equipment when necessary.

What can you do, then, to maintain gorgeous, healthy hair? To get you started, consider these suggestions:

Spend money on high-quality hair care items that are suitable for your hair type.

There are products available that can keep your hair healthy and looking its best whether it is dry, oily, or colored.

When shampooing your hair, stay away from hot water. Your hair may become dry and brittle if hot water is used to wash it. Instead, wash and rinse your hair with lukewarm or chilly water.

Regular hair trimming will help you avoid split ends and breakage. To maintain your hair healthy and looking its best, aim to trim it every 6 to 8 weeks.

Consume a balanced diet rich in vitamins and minerals to encourage the growth of good hair.

Finally, embrace the texture and style of your natural hair! Love the hair you were born with, whether it is straight, curly, or wavy, and rock it with pride.

Our bodies' important component of hair needs adequate maintenance to remain strong and attractive.

You can make sure that your hair looks amazing for years to come by creating a hair care routine and using the advice provided above!

You deserve it, so embrace your inner Rapunzel and let your hair down!

Homemade Treatments for Your Hair

Natural substances can be used to create a range of homemade hair treatments that can keep your hair healthy and beautiful. Here are few instances:

Coconut oil hair mask: Coconut oil is a great natural ingredient for moisturizing hair.

To make a hair mask, simply melt 1-2 tablespoons of coconut oil and apply it to your hair, focusing on the ends.

Leave the mask on for 30 minutes to an hour before washing it out with shampoo.

Avocado and egg hair mask: This hair mask is packed with protein and healthy fats to nourish and strengthen hair.

To make it, mash one ripe avocado and mix it with one beaten egg. Apply the mixture to your hair and let it sit for 20-30 minutes before rinsing it out with cool water.

Honey and olive oil hair mask: Honey is a natural humectant, meaning it helps to retain moisture in the hair. Olive oil is also great for moisturizing and conditioning hair.

To make this mask, mix together 2 tablespoons of honey and 3 tablespoons of olive oil. Apply the mixture to your hair and let it sit for 30 minutes before washing it out with shampoo.

Apple cider vinegar rinse: Apple cider vinegar helps to balance the pH of the scalp and can help remove buildup from hair products.

Mix one cup of water with 1-2 tablespoons of apple cider vinegar to create the rinse.

Pour the rinse over your hair after shampooing and conditioning it, then wait a few minutes before rinsing it out with cool water.

Aloe vera does wonders to calm the scalp and encourage hair development. Combine 2 teaspoons of aloe vera gel with 1 tablespoon of coconut oil to make a hair mask.

Apply the mixture to your hair, then wait 30 minutes before shampooing it out.

Without having to use harsh chemicals, these homemade hair treatments can be a terrific way to nurture and care for your hair.

The Dreading Shave!!!

Oh, the pleasures of being a girl growing up. You must not only adjust to the typical adolescent changes, but also master the art of shaving. But don't worry, with this shaving primer, we've got you covered!

Let's start by discussing the tools you'll need. A good razor, shaving cream or gel, and moisturizer are required.

For a close, smooth shave, it's crucial to select a razor made exclusively for ladies and equipped with many blades. Choose a soft and moisturizing shaving cream or gel, especially if you have sensitive skin.

Let's begin the actual shaving procedure now. To begin, take a warm bath or shower to soften your skin and hair.

This will ease shaving and lessen the chance of cuts and nicks. Make careful to properly cover the area with your shaving cream or gel before beginning to shave.

Shave with mild, delicate strokes in the direction of hair development while holding the razor at a 45-degree angle to the skin.

Never use too much pressure or shave the same region more than once because doing so might cause irritation and razor burn. To avoid clogging, frequently rinse the razor.

Rinse the region with lukewarm water after shaving to help shut the pores and lessen inflammation.

Apply a moisturizer after thoroughly drying the region with a clean towel to soothe the skin and stop it from drying out.

Let's now discuss several shaving blunders you should never do. Shaving against the direction of hair growth is one of the worst blunders since it can result in ingrown hairs and irritation.

Another error is using an outdated or dull razor, which can result in cuts and nicks. Shaving too frequently should also be avoided because it harms both the epidermis and hair follicles.

Don't freak out if you do get cuts or nicks while shaving! To stop the bleeding, press a clean tissue or cotton ball on the area.

To assist in stopping the bleeding and avoiding infection, you can also use an antiseptic or styptic pencil.

So there you have it—a tutorial to shaving for girls from scratch! You'll become an expert in no time with a little practice and the appropriate equipment.

Don't forget to take your time, be gentle, and pay attention to your body. Enjoy shaving!! Smiles

Did you hear about the razor that went to a party? It had a really sharp wit!

The Neat Feat

Keep Your Feet Neat: A Guide to Foot Care

Your feet expand as you do. One of your body's most crucial components, they transport you to your destinations, carry you through the day, and sustain your weight.

Your feet may grow weary and hurting from all the moving around, jogging, and leaping you perform. Consequently, it's crucial to look after them in order to keep them happy and healthy.

Here are some tips to keep your feet neat and feeling great:

Wash your feet daily

This is an essential part of foot hygiene. Wash your feet with warm water and soap every day to remove dirt and sweat.

Don't forget to dry them thoroughly, especially between the toes, to prevent fungal infections.

Keep your toenails trimmed

Trim your toenails straight across to prevent ingrown toenails. Don't cut them too short or too close to the skin, as this can cause pain and bleeding. Use a nail file to smooth out any rough edges.

Wear the right shoes

Wearing shoes that fit properly is important for foot health.

Make sure there is enough room for your toes to move freely and that the shoes provide good support for your feet.

Avoid wearing high heels for long periods of time, as they can cause pain and damage to your feet.

Take breaks and stretch

If you have to stand or sit for long periods of time, take breaks to stretch your legs and feet.

This can help improve circulation and reduce foot fatigue. You can also do foot exercises, such as toe curls and ankle rotations, to strengthen your feet and improve flexibility.

Use moisturizer

To keep your feet soft and smooth, apply moisturizer regularly, especially to dry or cracked areas. Avoid using moisturizer between the toes, as this can promote fungal growth.

Protect your feet

If you are participating in sports or other physical activities, wear proper footwear to protect your feet from injury.

You can also use foot pads or inserts to cushion your feet and absorb shock.

Seek medical attention for foot problems

Seek medical assistance if you have persistent foot pain, edema, or other issues.

It's critical to seek treatment right away because untreated foot issues can get worse over time.

These suggestions can help you maintain the health and happiness of your feet. So go ahead and maintain your tidy feet!

And keep in mind that a nice foot massage can always work miracles if everything else fails.

Insights about female feet include:

In general, women's feet are smaller than men's feet, with an average shoe size of 8.5.

Women are more likely than males to wear high heels and narrow-toed shoes, which increases their risk of developing foot issues like bunions, corns, and plantar fasciitis.

Since women's arches are typically higher than men's, they may experience more pain and discomfort in their feet.

Due to weight growth and hormonal changes, pregnancy can alter the feet, resulting in edema and a temporary rise in shoe size.

Because women's feet are often more flexible than men's feet, there is a higher chance of injury when engaging in physical activity.

Women frequently have more delicate foot soles than men, which makes them more sensitive to pain and suffering.

It's crucial to remember that these are generalizations and that not all ladies will have the same foot problems or exhibit the same features.

Wearing comfortable shoes that fit properly and taking care of your feet can help prevent foot issues and discomfort.

I Hate My Body!
It can be difficult to take care of your body, especially when it seems to be resisting you.

Being able to appreciate and feel confident in your own skin can be difficult when you have acne, stretch marks, or body hair.

But in actuality, everyone has at least one aspect of their physical appearance that they dislike.

Learning to accept and love oneself, flaws and all, is the key.

It's critical to keep in mind all the remarkable things your body accomplishes each day.

Your lungs keep you alive by breathing in and out, your heart beats without you even realizing it, and your brain manages every bodily process.

Not to be overlooked is your skin, which shields you from the damaging UV radiation and poisons in the environment.

But even with all these wonderful features, it's simple to concentrate on the drawbacks. It's possible that you have stubborn acne, self-conscious stretch marks, or hair in undesirable areas.

It's critical to keep in mind that you are not defined by these things. They are a component of who you are, but they do not entirely define who you are.

So how can you develop body love even when it's challenging? Here are some pointers:

Engage in self-care: One of the best ways to appreciate yourself is to take care of your body. This could entail engaging in regular exercise, obtaining enough sleep, or maintaining a healthy diet.

You'll feel better physically and mentally when you take care of your body.

Be in the company of positive people: It's simple to get into self-defeating thoughts, particularly if you're among people who are continuously critical of their own bodies.

People that uplift you and inspire you to love yourself should be all around you.

Challenge your negative thoughts: Make an effort to dispel any negative ideas you may have about your appearance.

For instance, if you tell yourself, "I hate my thighs," consider why you think so. Has someone stated anything to you that may be the cause?

Do you feel pressure to conform to a societal ideal as a result? Think differently and try to concentrate on the good things about your physique.

Embrace yourself: A little pampering occasionally goes a long way. Get a massage, a manicure, or a bubble bath for yourself. You'll feel more assured and at ease when you make time for yourself.

Embrace thankfulness: Every day, set aside some time to reflect on your blessings.

This could be anything from your devoted family and friends to your strong body that enables you to engage in the activities you enjoy.

Keep in mind that developing body love is a journey and not always simple.

But with time and effort, you may develop an appreciation for both your individuality and the incredible things your body is capable of.

Everybody has experienced those moments when they look in the mirror and wonder, "What is wrong with my body?

Perhaps you had a pimple the size of Mount Everest when you woke up, or your hair is curled in a manner that resembles a bird's nest.

Whatever it is, keep in mind that we all have those days and that it's acceptable to chuckle a little at ourselves.

Let's talk about those annoying hairs that always manage to grow in the most awkward places while we're on the subject of hair.

We all have hair in areas of our bodies that we wish we didn't, whether it's a stray hair on our chin or a patch of fuzz on our big toe.

The truth is that it goes beyond how we appear on the exterior. It has to do with how we internally feel.

And we feel good when we take good care of our body. We are assured. We feel strong. So let's discuss some strategies for loving our bodies despite the challenges.

Let's start by talking about exercise. You've heard it a gazillion times before, but bear with me. It's not just about looking nice while you exercise. It also involves feeling wonderful.

Our bodies produce endorphins during exercise, which are organic mood enhancers. Additionally, it promotes strength-building, which can increase our sense of strength and competence.

Now, I'm not telling you to start running marathons or anything like that.

Find a hobby you like, whether it's dancing, swimming, hiking, or even just going for a short stroll around the block. Your body should be moved in a way that feels natural to you.

Providing your body with nutritious meals is another way to show it love. Even though fast food is delectable, it's not good for our bodies.

A balanced diet rich in fresh produce, whole grains, lean protein, and other nutrients can offer us the energy we require to do our daily chores.

Of course, I'm not advocating that you never have a treat. Balance is the key.

Enjoy that cake, but also make sure you're giving your body the resources it requires to function.

Let's now discuss sleeping. Although binge-watching your favorite show till the wee hours of the morning can be tempting, getting adequate sleep is essential for our bodies to function effectively.

Increased stress, anger, and even weight gain can result from sleep deprivation. See how much better you feel by aiming for 7-8 hours of sleep each night.

Let's talk about self-care lastly. The important thing is to make time for yourself and do activities that make you feel good.

This can mean various things to different people.

Self-care may make us feel at ease, renewed, and prepared to face the world, whether it is taking a bubble bath, reading a book, or simply taking a few deep breaths.

There you have it, then. Although it's not always simple, it's crucial to love your body.

We may feel good on the inside and out by taking care of ourselves through exercise, a balanced diet, sleep, and self-care. Keep in mind that you are worth the work, and your body will appreciate it.

If everything else fails, keep in mind what my grandmother once said: "If you can't love yourself, how in the hell are you gonna love somebody else?" Can we all say "amen" up here?

What Kind of Body Do You Have, Anyway?
Are you curious about your body type?

Do you want to learn how to care for it in the best possible way?

Well, you're in luck, my friend! In this chapter, we're going to talk about the different body types and how you can take care of yours, whether you're a pear, an apple, or a banana (yes, you read that right).

First things first, let's take a look at the different body types:

The Pear: Do you have a tiny upper body and a voluptuous lower body, making you bottom-heavy? If so, congrats—you're a pear! This body type is prone to having fat deposits in the hips, thighs, and buttocks.

There's no need to worry, even though this may not be your ideal body type.

To balance out your proportions, embrace your curves and concentrate on toning your upper body.

The Apple: You have an apple-shaped body if you tend to carry more weight in your middle and your upper body is larger than your lower body.

A wider waistline and a flatter buttline define this body type. You can still look great with your body type even though you don't have pear-shaped curves by concentrating on developing a toned lower body and improving your posture.

The Banana: A banana-shaped body is one with little to no curves and a straight up-and-down figure.

This body type is characterized by a smaller breast and butt, as well as an even weight distribution across the body.

Even while you might wish you had your pear-shaped friends' curves, keep in mind that every body type has its own unique beauty.

Ensure that your muscles are toned, and use your attire to give the appearance of curves.

Now that you are aware of your body type, let's discuss how to care for it:

Exercise is crucial for keeping a healthy body, regardless of body type. Your body type, however, can influence the kind of activity you undertake.

Focus on upper body strength training if you are a pear to balance out your curves.

If you are an apple, reduce your waistline by combining lower body strength training with cardio workouts. If you're a banana, concentrate on toning your muscles to give the appearance of curves.

Diet Maintaining a healthy body requires eating a balanced diet. However, depending on your body type, other foods may be better for you to eat.

To balance their curves, pears should concentrate on eating more lean protein and healthy fats.

Apples should concentrate on increasing their intake of fruits and vegetables to assist reduce their belly fat.

To assist increase muscle tone, bananas should concentrate on consuming more complex carbohydrates.

Clothing: How you feel about your body can be greatly affected by the clothing you choose.

When choosing clothing, pears should emphasize their upper body by wearing V-neck tops and jackets that hit at the waist.

Apples should concentrate on donning clothing that accentuates the waistline, such as belted dresses and high-waisted slacks.

Bananas should concentrate on donning attire that gives the appearance of curves, including wrap dresses and ruffled shirts.

Folks, there you have it! It's time to accept your body and appreciate it for what it is now that you are aware of your body type and how to care for it.

Celebrate your body and all of its peculiarities since every body is different and lovely in its own way.!

Let's get serious now missy!

Ectomorph, mesomorph, and endomorph are the three fundamental body kinds, or somatotypes.

Each of these body types has unique traits and reacts differently to various exercise and dietary regimens. An overview of each somatotype is provided below:

Ectomorph: Ectomorphs often have short, slender bodies with long limbs. They frequently have a quick metabolism, which makes it challenging for them to put on weight or develop muscle.

Ectomorphs should concentrate on eating more calories than they expend while lifting weights and doing resistance training to increase their muscular mass.

Mesomorph: Mesomorphs often have a medium-sized frame, are athletic, and have a lot of muscle. Since they have a faster metabolism than endomorphs, they can put on muscle faster and burn more fat.

Mesomorphs should concentrate on maintaining their muscle bulk with training and a balanced diet.

Endomorph: Endomorphs often have larger frames, more body fat, and a stockier appearance.

They have a slower metabolism, which makes it more difficult for them to maintain a lean body or lose weight.

Endomorphs should concentrate on maintaining a nutritious diet and engaging in fat-burning cardiovascular workouts.

You can do a body type test online or speak with a fitness expert to ascertain your somatotype.

Knowing your body type will help you customize your diet and exercise program to better meet your demands.

Here's a fun quiz to determine your body type:

What is the shape of your face?

A. Round

B. Oval

C. Square

How would you describe your shoulders?

A. Rounded

B. Average width

C. Broad

How do you gain weight?

A. Easily, especially in the midsection

B. Gradually, all over

C. Hardly at all

How would you describe your waist?

A. Wide and undefined

B. Narrow and defined

C. Straight and similar to the hips

How would you describe your hips?

A. Narrow

B. Average

C. Wide

What is your body's natural shape?

A. Apple-shaped

B. Hourglass-shaped

C. Pear-shaped

What is the most prominent feature of your body?

A. Belly

B. Bust and hips

C. Thighs

How would you describe your legs?

A. Short and stout

B. Average length and toned

C. Long and slender

Now add up your answers:

Mostly A's: You have an apple-shaped body. This means your weight is concentrated in your midsection. To treat this body type, focus on exercises that strengthen your core and cardio exercises to burn fat.

Mostly B's: You have an hourglass-shaped body. This means your waist is significantly smaller than your bust and hips.

To treat this body type, focus on exercises that maintain your body's curves and proportion.

Mostly C's: Your physique is shaped like a pear. Your shoulders and bust are smaller than your hips, which indicates this.

Exercises that tone your lower body and strengthen your upper body should be your main focus while treating this body type.

No matter what kind of body you have, it's crucial to appreciate and take good care of it.

This include feeding it foods that are high in nutrients, being active, getting enough sleep, and abstaining from bad habits like smoking and binge drinking.

Try to concentrate on your blessings and the good parts of your physical and mental health if you're having trouble loving your body.

Regularly engage in self-care, and surround yourself with others who promote your wellbeing.

Keep in mind that your body is special and needs to be cherished and taken care of. Celebrate your uniqueness and the incredible things your body is capable of doing!

Yours Foodfully!

It's important to know how to take care of your body as a developing girl, and that includes learning how to feed it the correct foods.

It can be difficult to resist the temptation of junk food and sugary snacks, though, on sometimes. But fear not; you can make healthy eating enjoyable and exciting with a little information and imagination.

Let's start by discussing how important eating is for girls. Our bodies run on food, so it's important to fuel them with the right nutrients if we want to stay healthy and powerful.

To promote healthy growth and development, a balanced diet that includes a variety of foods is vital.

Let's move on to the exciting part, the food itself! Food that is healthy need not be bland and monotonous.

In fact, there are many of mouthwatering and wholesome options available that can sate your cravings and maintain the wellbeing of your body. Let's look at a few of them.

Fruits and Vegetables – These are the foundation of a healthy diet.

Aim to include a variety of fruits and vegetables in your meals and snacks to ensure that you're getting a range of vitamins, minerals, and fiber. Plus, they can be delicious and fun to eat.

Have you ever tried dipping apple slices in peanut butter or hummus? Yum!

Whole Grains – Choose whole-grain bread, pasta, and cereal instead of their refined counterparts. Whole grains contain more fiber and nutrients and can keep you feeling full and satisfied for longer.

Lean Protein – Protein is essential for building and repairing muscles, and it can also help keep you feeling full. Choose lean sources of protein, such as chicken, fish, beans, and tofu.

Healthy Fats – Fats are an essential part of a healthy diet, but it's essential to choose the right types. Opt for unsaturated fats found in nuts, seeds, avocado, and olive oil.

Water – Remember how important it is to drink enough of water! At least eight glasses of water should be consumed each day, while soda and fruit juice should be avoided.

After going over the fundamentals, let's talk about ways to make eating healthy enjoyable and interesting. Using your imagination in the kitchen is one method to do this.

Test out new recipes and play around with flavors and ingredients. You can do it jointly as a pleasant pastime with your friends or family.

Making minor adjustments and substitutions to your favorite meals is another approach to make healthy eating enjoyable.

If you enjoy pizza, for instance, consider creating your own with a whole-wheat crust and loads of vegetables.

If you have a sweet tooth, try substituting fruit or dark chocolate for sugary snacks.

Remember that moderation and balance are the keys to a healthy diet. It's acceptable to occasionally indulge in your favorite foods, but strive to make healthy decisions the majority of the time.

Remember to pay attention to your body's cues and eat only when you are hungry and stop when you are full.

With a little preparation and imagination, girls and food can make for a delightful and amusing combo.

You may nurture your body and keep it happy and healthy by making tiny tweaks to your favorite meals and a range of healthy foods.

So go ahead and experiment with some new dishes and relish the flavorful path toward a healthy diet!

Food for You on the Go
Healthy Eating for Girls on the Go

Hello, busy bees! Do you frequently find yourself racing from one task to the next, barely having time to catch your breath, let alone stop and get a nutritious meal?

So, do not worry! You may still provide your body with the healthy nourishment it requires to keep you running all day long with a little advance preparation and innovative thinking.

First things first, let's discuss the significance of a healthy diet. Even though that greasy pizza slice may taste delicious at the time, it won't provide you with the sustained energy you need to go through the rest of the day.

Maintaining a healthy weight, enhancing your mood, and even increasing your mental capacity can all be achieved by eating a balanced diet rich in fruits, vegetables, whole grains, and lean protein.

So let's get started with some suggestions for eating well while on the run.

First-rate Snack Advice We've all experienced the sensation of being hungry, which causes us to go for the nearby bag of chips or candy bar.

However, those ineffective calories won't benefit you in the long run. Instead, choose snacks like a handful of almonds, a piece of fruit, or some carrot sticks with hummus that will provide you with long-lasting energy.

And when you're on the run, remember to bring some food with you so you won't be tempted by the vending machine.

Tip #2: Make a plan. Spend some time the night before organizing your meals and snacks when you know you'll have a busy day.

Perhaps you could prepare some overnight oats to pick up on your way out the door or pack a lunch to take to work or school.

You can avoid the temptation to go for something unhealthy in a fit of hunger by having healthy options on hand.

Tip #3: When Dining Out, Choose Wisely Sometimes it's impossible to avoid eating out, whether it's at a sit-down restaurant or a fast food outlet. But that doesn't imply you should abandon your sensible eating practices.

Instead of fried food, look for menu items that are grilled, roasted, or steamed.

Also, don't be hesitant to request changes, such as asking for dressing on the side or exchanging fries for a side salad.

#4: Drink plenty of water. Water consumption is essential for general health and can even make you feel more focused and alert.

Additionally, as thirst is sometimes mistaken for hunger, staying hydrated might aid in preventing overeating.

Try to drink at least 8 cups of water each day, and always carry a reusable water bottle with you.

Tip #5: Be Kind to Yourself (Moderately) you can still enjoy your favorite pleasures if you consume a balanced diet.

Actually, giving yourself a treat now and then might keep you on track with your healthy eating routine. Just remember to consume these sweets in moderation and counterbalance them with a variety of nourishing foods.

You now have some advice on how to eat healthfully even if you are constantly on the run, ladies.

Keep in mind that feeding your body with healthy foods is worth the effort because taking care of your body is crucial.

Therefore, grab a healthy snack the next time you're rushing out the door and face the day with confidence!

Here's a timeline and some examples for healthy eating for girls:

Breakfast (7-8 am):

Oatmeal with fruits, nuts and honey

Greek yogurt with berries and granola

Avocado toast with a boiled egg

Mid-morning snack (10-11 am):

Apple slices with almond butter

Hummus with carrots and celery sticks

Trail mix with dried fruits and nuts

Lunch (12-1 pm):

Grilled chicken salad with mixed greens, veggies and a vinaigrette dressing

Quinoa bowl with roasted veggies, chickpeas and a tahini sauce

Whole wheat wrap with turkey, avocado, veggies and mustard

Afternoon snack (3-4 pm):

Banana with peanut butter

Rice cakes with hummus and cucumber slices

Smoothie with banana, spinach, almond milk and protein powder

Dinner (6-7 pm):

Baked salmon with roasted sweet potatoes and broccoli

Brown rice stir-fry with tofu, mixed veggies and soy sauce

Grilled chicken with quinoa and grilled asparagus

Evening snack (8-9 pm):

Greek yogurt with honey and cinnamon

Popcorn with nutritional yeast

Dark chocolate with almonds

Remember to also drink plenty of water throughout the day and limit sugary drinks like soda and juice.

With a balanced diet and healthy eating habits, you can fuel your body and feel your best.

Smart Choices for Fast Food

For individuals who are constantly on the go, fast food is a necessity in many people's lives.

It is well known that fast food isn't necessarily the healthiest choice, though. But do not worry; there are healthier options available that will still satiate your needs without endangering your health.

Start by avoiding fried meals. Although appealing, fried chicken, French fries, and onion rings are high in harmful fats and calories.

Choose grilled chicken or fish instead, and if you must have fries, choose baked or air-fried varieties.

Next, keep an eye out for sugary beverages. Even though they may taste delicious, sodas and milkshakes are high in sugar and empty calories.

Change to low-fat milk, unsweetened tea, or water as an alternative.

Make informed decisions when it comes to burgers. Choose a single-patty burger or even a veggie burger instead of the double- or triple-patty options.

Skip the mayo and other high-calorie toppings and pile on the vegetables.

Choose grilled chicken or fish tacos over the fried varieties if you're in the mood for Mexican food. For taste without too many calories, pile on the salsa and guacamole.

Finally, pay attention to serving sizes. Consider splitting a meal with a friend or choosing a lesser size because fast food portions are frequently rather enormous.

Just keep in mind that occasionally indulging in fast food won't ruin your otherwise healthy eating routine. Just be conscious of your decisions, and whenever you can, choose wisely.

Here are some smart choices to make when it comes to fast food:

- Pick grilled or baked foods over fried ones: When it comes to meat, choose grilled or baked chicken or fish over fried foods like fish and chips or chicken nuggets. This will assist in lowering the number of calories and bad fats in your diet.

- Ditch the fries: If you're ordering a meal with a side of fries, substitute a side salad, fruit cup, or veggie sticks for something healthy.

- Be aware of portion sizes: A lot of fast food places serve super-sized dishes that contain more food than you can eat at one time. To keep your meals in check, think about ordering a smaller dish or splitting a meal with a friend.

- Steer clear of sugary beverages: These can significantly increase the calorie content of your meal without adding any nutritious value. Choose water, unsweetened iced tea, or a small carton of low-fat milk as an alternative.

- Include some vegetables: Try to include some vegetables in your meal, either as a side dish or by selecting options like salads or wraps that are made with vegetables. This will increase the meal's nutritional content and add some fiber to make you feel more satisfied.

- Examine the nutrition facts: Nowadays, a lot of fast food businesses offer nutrition facts for their menu items online or in-store. Check the calories and fat content of the products you're thinking about for a few minutes so you can make a more informed decision..

Although everyone enjoys fast food, it's not necessarily the healthiest choice. However, you are not have to give up your favorite burgers and fries. Simply choose wiser options when you're ordering.

This is why: After consuming a triple bacon cheeseburger, have you ever attempted to run a marathon?

It isn't pretty, I assure you. Your stomach will be turning while you are gasping for air and attempting to catch your breath.

You'll feel energized and prepared to take on the world if you choose a grilled chicken sandwich with a side salad, though. Maybe even set a new record for yourself. The future?

A healthier fast food alternative will also leave you with extra room for dessert, so consider that! And who doesn't enjoy dessert, let's face it?

Don't be frightened to make a wise decision the next time you're in the drive-through. Your body, taste buds, and marathon time will all appreciate it.

Why am I Weight Worried?

Do you have concerns about your weight? It's not just you. Many young women worry about their weight and frequently experience pressure to maintain a certain appearance.

The good news is that it's not difficult or constrained to keep a healthy weight. In this post, we'll look at some entertaining and helpful pointers for keeping a healthy weight.

Why Weight Matters: Let's first discuss why weight matters before moving on to the advice.

Many factors make it crucial to maintain a healthy weight. First and foremost, it can aid in the prevention of illnesses including high blood pressure, diabetes, and heart disease.

Additionally, having a healthy weight can increase your self-esteem and confidence, which will make you happier and lead to a more satisfying existence.

Tip #1: Concentrate on Whole meals Eating whole meals is one of the best things you can do for your weight (and general health).

When it comes to nutrition and fiber, whole foods are those that are as close to their original form as possible. Fruits, vegetables, whole grains, lean proteins, and healthy fats are a few examples of entire foods.

Second advice: Mind your portions When it comes to maintaining a healthy weight, portion control is essential.

Even if you eat nutritious meals, overindulging in them might make you gain weight. Try weighing or measuring your meals to make sure you're getting the proper amount to eat.

One serving of protein should be the size of your palm, one serving of carbs should be the size of your fist, and one serving of fat should be the size of your thumb.

You can also use the "hand method" to estimate quantities.

Move Your Body (**Tip #3**) An essential component of keeping a healthy weight is exercise. However, it does not follow that you must work out for several hours each day.

Find activities you want to do and include them into your schedule. That may be taking a walk after dinner, enrolling in a dance class, or participating in a sport with friends.

Tip #4: Make mindful eating a habit Being mindful while eating is the key to successful mindful eating. In order to do this, you should pay attention to your hunger and fullness cues, eat deliberately, and relish your meals.

You'll be more likely to eat when you're hungry and stop when you're full if you practice mindful eating, which can help you avoid overeating.

Tip #5: Don't Deprive Yourself

 Finally, it's critical to keep in mind that a balanced diet is the key to good health. As long as you're using moderation, it's alright to occasionally indulge in your favorite foods.

Depriving yourself of your favorite foods can make you feel restricted and ultimately cause you to overeat.

Why weight is irrelevant After discussing some advice for maintaining a healthy weight, let's discuss why weight isn't as important as we might believe.

The truth is that your weight is only a number; it has no bearing on your value as a person.

It's crucial to keep in mind that every person has a unique body, so what works for one person could not work for another. Instead than focusing just on the scale's reading, pay attention to how you physically and mentally feel.

Particularly throughout puberty when their bodies are developing quickly, many girls worry about their weight.

But don't worry, we're here to dispel some widespread misconceptions about obesity and assist you in making healthier decisions.

Myth 1: To be happy, you must be skinny.

False! Happiness stems from the within, not from how big or how small you are. Regardless of your weight, your body is special and lovely. You'll feel better overall if you put more effort into caring for your physical and emotional well-being.

Myth No. 2: Crash diets are the best option.

Without a doubt! Although crash diets may seem like a quick remedy, they are neither healthful nor lasting. They might even be harmful and cause nutrient deficits.

Instead, focus on making incremental, long-term adjustments to your food and lifestyle.

Myth #3: Carbohydrates are harmful

Mistake again! A healthy diet should include enough of carbohydrates since they give your body energy.

The secret is to select complex carbohydrates like whole grains, fruits, and vegetables over simple carbohydrates like sweetened beverages and snacks.

Myth No.4: Missing meals might help you lose weight.

Nope! In fact, skipping meals might have the opposite effect and make your body store fat as a defense strategy. Additionally, it may cause later overeating.

To keep your metabolism active, aim to consume smaller, more frequent meals throughout the day.

For your general health and wellbeing, it's crucial to maintain a healthy weight, but doing so doesn't have to be difficult or stressful.

You can achieve and retain a healthy weight by concentrating on nutritious meals, controlling your portions, moving your body, practicing mindful eating, and not depriving yourself.

Remember that how you feel on the inside and out is more important than how much you weigh.

And hey, if all else fails, keep in mind that ice cream and pizza are still delectable, regardless of what the scale indicates. ☺

Girls and Sports
Girls Just Wanna Have Fun: The Importance of Sports

Hey, ladies! Are you prepared to work out, have fun, and grow more powerful? If not, it is now time to begin. Sports are a fantastic way to make friends and have a good time, in addition to being a terrific way to remain fit.

This chapter will cover the value of sports, how to get started, and some of the top activities for female athletes.

Let's start by discussing the reasons why sports are so amazing. They're a wonderful way to remain in shape, for starters.

And when you're strong and healthy, you'll feel more self-assured and up to facing the world. Additionally, participating in sports allows you to practice a variety of skills, including coordination, stamina, and speed.

But sports are not just about physical conditioning. They're a fantastic way to socialize and develop a sense of community.

Being on a team allows you to cooperate towards a common objective while also teaching you to rely on and support one another.

Sports are also a terrific opportunity to meet new people and form connections even if you're not on a team.

I'm not athletic, you might be saying. Sports are not my thing. The truth is that anyone may participate in sports. Being the best, the quickest, or the strongest is not the point. It's about pushing yourself to be the best version of yourself while enjoying the journey.

So, how do you begin? Finding a sport you enjoy playing is the first stage, of course. There are numerous choices, ranging from team sports like basketball and soccer to solitary activities like running and yoga.

Explore a few options and decide what feels comfortable for you. Also, don't stress if you don't succeed straight away. Keep in mind that everyone has a beginning.

It's crucial to continue participating in your favorite sport after you've found it. Schedule it and give it the same importance as you would any other critical task.

And don't be reluctant to create objectives for yourself. Perhaps you want to practice your cartwheels or run a 5k. Whatever it may be, having something to strive for may be really inspiring.

So which sports are the best for girls? Listed here are some of our favorites:

Soccer is a fantastic team activity that emphasizes coordination and stamina. Additionally, kicking a ball around with your pals is a lot of fun.

Yoga is a fantastic choice if you're looking for something a little more sedate. It's all about power and flexibility, and it may be a terrific way to unwind.

Swimming is a fantastic solo activity that engages your entire body. Additionally, it's a fantastic way to escape the summer heat.

Dance is a wonderful way to move and express yourself, whether you're into ballet, hip hop, or something in between.

You might be asking, "But what about all the sweat, the mess, and the grossness?" and we understand. Sports can indeed be dirty. Yes, you may perspire. Yes, it's possible that you'll trip or get a little dirty. But here's the thing—all of that is fun. You don't worry about appearing or acting flawless while you play sports. You're just being yourself and having fun.

Sports can play a critical part in assisting females manage the considerable changes their bodies go through during puberty.

The rapid growth in body size and weight that happens throughout puberty is one of the biggest changes that happens.

By burning extra calories and gaining lean muscle mass, sports can assist girls in maintaining a healthy weight and body composition.

Sports are beneficial for bone health as well. Girls' bone mass increases during puberty, and regular exercise can aid in developing and maintaining strong, healthy bones.

Girls should pay special attention to this since they are more likely than boys to develop osteoporosis later in life.

Sports can improve one's physical and mental health in addition to their physical benefits.

Endorphins, which are released when you exercise regularly, can elevate mood, lessen tension and anxiety, and increase self-esteem.

In addition, playing sports gives girls the chance to form friendships, hone their leadership and collaboration abilities, and learn how to deal with and overcome obstacles.

These are essential life skills that girls can use all their lives.

In general, sports are a vital part of a healthy lifestyle for girls going through adolescence.

Sports can support girls' confidence and resilience as they face the challenges of puberty by fostering their physical, mental, and social well-being.

What are you still holding out for? Get those sneakers on, grab a drink, and head outside to play! Sports aren't just about staying fit, keep that in mind.

Sports, Safety and You!

Girls are tough, let's face it. They are skilled athletes who can play any sport.

However, enormous authority also entails great responsibility. While you're out there dominating on the field or court, it's crucial to ensure your safety.

We'll discuss some sports safety advice for girls in this chapter.

Wear the Right Gear

Make sure you have the appropriate equipment for your sport before anything else. Injuries can be avoided by donning the proper footwear, helmets, pads, gloves, and clothing.

Before every practice or game, you should make sure your equipment is in good working order.

Warm-Up and Cool Down

It's necessary to warm up and cool down before and after participating in sports. This can help you avoid injuries and maintain excellent physical condition.

Stretching, brisk walking, or even a quick game of catch might be used as warm-ups. Walking around or stretching once more can serve as a basic form of cooling off.

Stay Hydrated

Drinking enough water is crucial when playing sports. Dehydration can lead to cramps, fatigue, and even heat exhaustion. Make sure to drink water before, during, and after playing sports.

Follow the Rules

Rules exist for a reason. They're there to keep you and other players safe.

Make sure to follow the rules of your sport and always play fair. Don't take unnecessary risks or try to cheat, as it can lead to injuries.

Listen to Your Body

If something hurts or feels off, listen to your body. Don't ignore pain or try to "push through" it. Rest, ice, and seek medical attention if needed. It's better to take a break and recover than to risk making an injury worse.

Have Fun!

Most importantly, remember to have fun! Playing sports can be a great way to stay active, make friends, and relieve stress. Don't take it too seriously, and enjoy the game!

So, whether you're a soccer star, a basketball champ, or a track and field pro, remember to stay safe while playing sports.

Follow these tips, and you'll be sure to crush it on the field or court while also keeping your body in top shape.

Girls and Eating Disorders

We're going to discuss eating disorders today, which is a slightly serious but still very essential subject.

Let's be clear about one thing before we continue: we are all special and lovely in our ways. We should be happy that we are all diverse forms and sizes!

Sadly, there are instances when society puts pressure on us to maintain a specific appearance, which might result in some bad habits. Eating disorders get into that.

Let's define what an eating disorder is first. In reality, they are a collection of ailments involving poor eating and body image.

Anorexia nervosa, bulimia nervosa, and binge eating disorder are a few examples of common eating disorders.

People with anorexia nervosa severely restrict their food intake, frequently to the point of starving. Malnutrition and other severe health problems may result from this.

People who frequently engage in binge eating episodes and then engage in purging activities, such as vomiting or taking laxatives, are said to have bulimia nervosa.

People with binge eating disorders frequently have episodes of binge eating without engaging in any purge practices.

The truth is that anyone can develop an eating disorder, regardless of gender, age, or body type. Nevertheless, a few things can make you more likely to get an eating disorder.

People who have experienced trauma or abuse in the past or who have a family history of eating disorders, for instance, maybe more vulnerable.

Social and cultural pressures to conform to a particular body type or weight are another element that may be at play.

So, how may eating disorders be avoided? The secret is to adopt healthy behaviors and accept yourself as you are. Here are a few advice:

Ensure that you are feeding your body nutritious nutrients. This entails maintaining a balanced diet rich in fresh produce, whole grains, lean protein, and other nutrients.

Eat according to intuition. Eat when you're hungry and stop when you're full by paying attention to your body's hunger and fullness cues.

Don't assess yourself against others. There is no such thing as a "perfect" figure because we are all special and attractive in our ways.

Try to surround yourself with uplifting people. This entails avoiding individuals who bring you down and spending time with those that uplift and support you.

Just keep in mind that everyone is amazing and deserving of love and respect.

Let's adopt healthy behaviors and encourage one another as we work to take care of our bodies.

Move It, Shake, Have Fun

We'll discuss ways to move your body even when you just want to curl up with your phone and watch your favorite show in its entirety. I understand, I promise.

But because we are all aware of the benefits of exercise to both our physical and mental health, let's look for enjoyable methods to move!

First of all, it's crucial to keep in mind that "movement" refers to more than just going to the gym and running for an hour on a treadmill.

There are so many other activities you can do to increase your heart rate and move your body instead than sitting in front of a wall of TVs and trying not to perspire. Here are a few instances:

Dance it out! Whether you're into hip hop, ballet, or just plain goofing around in your bedroom, dancing is a great way to get your body moving and your blood pumping.

Plus, it's way more fun than jogging on a treadmill. Blast your favorite music and dance like nobody's watching!

Take a hike. Literally. Grab some friends or family members and hit the trails for a day of exploring and fresh air.

Not only is hiking great exercise, but it's also a great way to connect with nature and get some much-needed Vitamin D.

Play a sport. Don't worry, you don't have to be a superstar athlete to enjoy a game of pick-up basketball or a friendly round of frisbee. Just get out there and have fun with it!

Not only will you be getting exercise, but you'll also be practicing teamwork and sportsmanship.

Try a new fitness class. There are countless options, including kickboxing, yoga, and Zumba!

Furthermore, enrolling in a class is a terrific chance to meet new people and put yourself through a fun challenge.

I'm aware of your thoughts at this point. But wait, won't performing some of these things make me look foolish? Let me let you in on a little secret: while doing anything new, everyone looks foolish.

You know what's even more absurd, though? Spending the entire day on the couch, wishing you were more active but being too terrified to try anything new.

Therefore, focus more on having fun and feeling confident in your own skin than trying to look hip.

Let's talk about the advantages of staying active while we're on the subject of feeling good in your own skin.

Regular exercise has been demonstrated to improve mental health in addition to maintaining physical health and strength.

Endorphins, which naturally elevate mood, are released when you exercise.

Additionally, you're more likely to feel secure and in control of your life in general when you feel good about your body and what it is capable of.

So let's review: being physically active doesn't have to be a chore or uninteresting.

Make a habit of doing anything you like to do, whether it's dancing, hiking, playing a sport, or attending a fitness class.

And keep in mind that having fun and feeling good about yourself are the most essential things. So venture outside and start moving!

A Little Sleep is not enough

Ah, SLEEP. That one thing that we all adore yet can never get enough of.

The proper quantity of sleep is crucial for the physical and mental wellbeing of a growing girl.

In actuality, getting adequate sleep is just as crucial as maintaining a good diet and doing regular exercise.

But why, you might wonder, is sleep so crucial? Let's get started and find out.

Sleep is crucial for your body to renew and restore itself. Your body produces growth hormone when you sleep, which aids in tissue regeneration and repair.

This is particularly crucial throughout puberty because your body is changing significantly and needs all the support it can get to grow and develop normally.

Your mental health is also greatly affected by how well you sleep. Increased feelings of anxiety, anger, and despair can result from sleep deprivation.

Contrarily, getting enough sleep can lift your spirits, make you feel more alert and focused, and even help you remember things better.

What amount of sleep do you actually require? Well, that depends on your age and specific requirements.

Teenagers often require 8 to 10 hours of sleep every night. Teenagers' specific needs may dictate whether they require more or less than this.

After establishing the value of sleep, let's discuss some suggestions for getting a good night's sleep.

Maintain a consistent sleeping routine. Even on weekends, try to keep your bedtime and wakeup times consistent.

Make a space that promotes rest. Ensure that it is cool, quiet, and dark in your bedroom. To eliminate distractions, think about employing white noise machines or blackout curtains.

Prior to going to bed, avoid caffeine and sugar. Both have the potential to disturb your sleep and keep you awake at night.

Relax before going to bed. To unwind and get ready for bed, take a warm bath, read a book, or play relaxing music.

Restrict your screen time before bed. Electronic device blue light can interfere with your body's normal sleep-wake cycle and make it more difficult for you to go to sleep.

Does sleep really crucial for academic performance, as the age-old debate goes? Even though it hurts, your parents were right when they advised you to get a good night's sleep before a significant test.

Why? To begin with, fatigue causes your brain to function less optimally.

Similar like trying to drive a car with a flat tire, you might be able to get it moving, but you won't be taking first place in any competitions.

However, when you're well-rested, your mind is clear-headed, attentive, and prepared to take on any academic obstacle that comes your way.

That's not all, though. Lack of sleep makes it more difficult for the brain to remember things.

No matter how hard you try, some water will always manage to leak through the cracks in a bucket that is trying to hold water.

However, when you get enough sleep, your brain is like a strong bucket that is prepared to hold onto every bit of information you pour into it.

Another interesting fact is that having adequate sleep can really improve your creativity.

Yes, your brain is more equipped to form novel connections and generate original thoughts when you are well-rested.

So make sure you're well-rested before attempting to compose a stellar essay or come up with a creative project proposal.

Of course, I'm not claiming that getting enough sleep is essential for doing well in school.

Numerous other elements also play a role, such as consistently studying, maintaining organization, and seeking assistance when necessary.

However, getting enough sleep is a wonderful place to start if you're searching for a quick and efficient strategy to give yourself a competitive edge in the classroom.

So feel free to use the snooze button once again. It will benefit both your brain and your academic performance.

Keep in mind that obtaining adequate sleep is essential for both your physical and mental well-being. So, prioritize it, and good night!

Having a Goodnight Sleep

Your physical and mental health depend on getting a decent night's sleep, and as we have mentioned, it can improve your academic performance.

However, what if you have problems getting to sleep or remaining asleep? We have some advice to assist you get those elusive Zzzs, so don't worry!

Follow a sleeping schedule: Even on weekends, try to keep your bedtime and wakeup times consistent. This can hasten your ability to fall asleep by regulating the biological clock in your body.

Establish a bedtime schedule: Establish a tranquil bedtime routine that includes activities like a warm bath, reading, or listening to soothing music.

Your brain may receive this as a cue to relax and get ready for sleep.

Keep the room calm, dark, and cool: Keep your bedroom cold, quiet, and dark to create a sleeping environment that is conducive to rest. If you reside in a noisy setting, think about utilizing earplugs or a white noise machine.

Avoid using gadgets and coffee before bed: Avoid consuming caffeine in the late afternoon or evening because it is a stimulant that can keep you awake.

Additionally, utilizing electronics like cellphones and computers before bed can interfere with your sleep due to the blue light they emit.

Regular exercise is good for your general health and can improve your ability to sleep at night.

Just be sure to conclude your exercise session a few hours before bedtime because exercising too soon before bed can actually make it harder to fall asleep.

Try some relaxation techniques: You can relax and go to sleep more quickly by using methods like progressive muscle relaxation, deep breathing, and meditation.

You may find numerous applications and tutorials that will walk you through these procedures.

Avoid taking naps during the day: Even though it may be tempting, especially if you didn't get enough sleep the night before, taking a nap during the day can make it more difficult to fall asleep at night.

Try to keep naps to 20 to 30 minutes and take them earlier in the day if you really need to.

Never forget that obtaining a good night's sleep is important for your health and happiness as well as for your academic performance. So put your electronics away, put on your coziest pajamas, and good night!

CHAPTER THREE

FRIENDS AND FEELINGS

We will examine sentiments and friends in this chapter. Understanding your emotions and how they affect your friendships with your pals is crucial for young girls.

We'll discuss various approaches to managing your emotions and keeping healthy friendships.

Do you feel overwhelmed? It's Not Just You: It's common to experience occasional overwhelm.

Your emotions might be affected by work, home life, and social interactions. To avoid feeling overwhelmed, it's crucial to learn how to control these emotions. Here are some suggestions to assist you:

Go on a break: The greatest course of action is occasionally to stand back and relax. Find a relaxing and distracting activity, whether it be reading a book, listening to music, or taking a walk.

Speak with someone: It's acceptable to seek assistance. Speak to a friend, relative, or guidance counselor at your school.

They can lend a sympathetic ear and offer advice on how to deal with your feelings.

Note this down: Writing down your ideas and emotions might occasionally be a good way to process them. Try journaling or composing a letter (even if you don't intend to send it) to someone.

The Value of Strong Friendships: Your emotional wellness depends on having a strong social network. But what exactly does a solid friendship entail? These traits are listed:

Trust: Trust is the foundation of any healthy relationship. You should feel comfortable confiding in your friend and know that they won't judge you.

Respect: A healthy friendship involves mutual respect. You should feel respected and valued by your friend, and you should treat them with the same level of respect.

Communication: Communication is key in any relationship, including friendships. You and your friend should feel comfortable expressing your thoughts and feelings to each other.

Support: A healthy friend will support you through good times and bad. They will be there for you when you need them and celebrate your successes.

Dealing with Conflict: Unfortunately, conflict is inevitable in any relationship. However, it's how you handle it that makes a difference. Here are some tips for dealing with conflict:

Listen: When a conflict arises, take the time to listen to the other person's perspective. Try to see things from their point of view.

Communicate: Express your thoughts and feelings calmly and respectfully. Avoid getting defensive or attacking the other person.

Find a solution: Work together to find a solution that works for both of you. Be willing to compromise and find a middle ground.

Forgive and move on: Holding onto grudges will only make the situation worse. Learn to forgive and move on from the conflict.

It's essential to understand your feelings and how they impact your relationships with your friends.

Learning how to manage your emotions and maintain healthy friendships, you'll be able to navigate the ups and downs of adolescence successfully.

Remember, it's okay to ask for help, and a healthy friendship involves trust, respect, communication, and support.

Becoming Your Own Boss

Hey there, boss lady! Welcome to the section where we talk about being the boss of YOU. That's right, no one else gets to make decisions for you, but you.

You are in control of your own life, your own feelings, and your own future. So let's dive in and talk about what it means to be the boss of you.

First things first, let's talk about your feelings. Sometimes, it can feel like your feelings are controlling you. You might feel angry, sad, or frustrated for no reason at all.

But remember, you are the boss of your feelings, not the other way around. Here are a few tips to help you be the boss of your emotions:

Identify your feelings: Take a moment to think about how you're feeling. Are you angry? Sad? Frustrated? Identifying your emotions can help you better understand them and take control.

Find a way to express your emotions: Whether it's talking to a friend, writing in a journal, or drawing a picture, finding a way to express your emotions can help you release them and feel better.

Take a break: Sometimes, you just need to take a break from a situation or a person that is causing you stress or negative emotions. It's okay to take a step back and regroup.

Now let's talk about being the boss of your own life. You have the power to make decisions that will impact your future. Here are a few tips to help you take control:

Set goals: What do you want to achieve in life? Whether it's getting good grades, learning a new skill, or pursuing a passion, setting goals can help you stay motivated and focused.

Make a plan: Once you've set your goals, make a plan to achieve them. Break them down into smaller, achievable steps and track your progress along the way.

Surround yourself with positive influences: The people you surround yourself with can have a big impact on your life. Choose friends who support and encourage you, and avoid those who bring you down.

Remember, being the boss of you is all about taking control of your own life and emotions.

It's not always easy, but with a little practice and determination, you can be the boss lady of your own life!

When it comes to making the right decisions, think of yourself as a superhero with a superpower that allows you to control your destiny.

It's like being in a choose-your-own-adventure book, except the choices you make will have a real impact on your life.

Let's say you're at a crossroads and you have two choices: you can either study for your upcoming exam or binge-watch the latest season of your favorite show.

If you choose to study, you'll probably do well on your exam and feel proud of yourself for being responsible.

But if you choose to binge-watch your show, you might feel good in the moment, but later on, you'll feel stressed and overwhelmed because you didn't prepare properly.

Making the right decisions also means thinking about the long-term.

Sure, eating that extra slice of pizza might feel amazing right now, but how will you feel tomorrow when your stomach is upset and you don't feel your best?

On the other hand, choosing to eat a healthy meal might not be as exciting in the moment, but you'll feel energized and ready to take on the day.

The bottom line is that making the right decisions may not always be the most fun or exciting option, but it will ultimately lead to a better future.

So go ahead, channel your inner superhero and make those decisions that will lead you to success!

Making and Keeping Friends (Your Best Shot)

Hey there, social butterflies! Are you tired of being a lone wolf? Are you ready to spread your wings and make some new friends?

Well, you've come to the right place! In this chapter, we'll be talking about the dos and don'ts of making friends.

First things first, let's address the elephant in the room. Making friends can be tough.

You put yourself out there, only to be met with awkward silences and forced small talk. It's enough to make you want to crawl back into your shell and never come out.

But fear not, my shy little sunflowers! Making friends doesn't have to be hard, and it can actually be a lot of fun.

Tip #1: Be yourself, unless you're a vampire. In that case, maybe hold off on the bloodsucking talk until you've gotten to know someone a little better.

But seriously, don't try to be someone you're not just to impress someone else. It's exhausting and unsustainable.

Tip #2: Step out of your comfort zone. I know, I know. It's called a comfort zone for a reason. But if you want to make new friends, you need to be willing to try new things and meet new people.

Maybe you join a club or take a class that interests you. Or maybe you just strike up a conversation with that person sitting next to you on the bus.

You never know where a new friendship might come from.

Tip #3: Be a good listener. We all love talking about ourselves, but sometimes the best way to make a friend is to be a good listener.

Ask questions, show interest in what they're saying, and don't interrupt. You'll be surprised at how quickly people open up when they feel heard.

Tip #4: Don't be afraid to be the one to make plans. If you hit it off with someone, don't wait around for them to ask you to hang out. Take the initiative and make the first move.

Maybe invite them to a movie or suggest grabbing lunch together. You'll come across as confident and fun, and they'll appreciate your willingness to take charge.

Tip #5: Be patient. Rome wasn't built in a day, and neither are friendships. It takes time to build trust and create a bond with someone.

Don't get discouraged if it takes a little while to find your friend soul mate. In the meantime, enjoy the journey and the new experiences that come with it.

So there you have it, folks! Making friends doesn't have to be scary or overwhelming. Just be yourself, step out of your comfort zone, listen well, take initiative, and be patient.

And remember, life's too short for boring friends. So get out there and find your tribe! Have you ever heard the phrase "no man is an island?" Well, it's true! Humans are social creatures, and friendships can have a huge impact on our lives.

Not only do they make life more fun, but they can also have some pretty significant benefits on the long run.

For starters, friends can provide emotional support during tough times.

Whether you're going through a break-up or dealing with a family issue, having friends who are there to listen and offer advice can be invaluable.

Plus, they can make you laugh and distract you from your problems for a little while.

But the benefits don't stop there. Research has shown that people with strong social connections tend to live longer, healthier lives.

Having friends can lower your stress levels and boost your immune system, both of which can help you stay healthy in the long run.

And let's not forget about the practical benefits of friendships. Your friends might be able to help you out with job connections or give you a ride when your car breaks down.

They can also introduce you to new people and experiences that you might not have had access to otherwise.

Of course, making friends isn't always easy, especially as you get older. But the effort is worth it.

And remember, it's never too late to make new friends. Join a club or a sports team, take a class, or volunteer for a cause that you're passionate about.

You never know who you might meet and what kind of impact they could have on your life.

So go ahead and make those friends! Not only will they make life more enjoyable, but they can also have some pretty significant benefits on the long run.

And who knows, maybe they'll be the ones to bail you out when you need a getaway driver...just kidding (kind of).

Friendship Skills (How to make'em)

Friendships are a big part of our lives. They bring joy, laughter, and a sense of belonging.

However, building and maintaining friendships can be challenging, especially as we grow older and our lives become more complex. That's why it's essential to develop strong friendship skills.

So, what are friendship skills? Friendship skills are the abilities and qualities that help us form and maintain healthy relationships with others. Some of these skills include:

Communication: Being able to express yourself clearly and actively listen to others is key to building strong friendships.

Misunderstandings can happen, so it's important to communicate effectively and openly to avoid any miscommunication.

Empathy: Putting yourself in your friend's shoes can help you understand their perspective and build deeper connections.

It's essential to show empathy towards your friends and try to understand their feelings and experiences.

Trustworthiness: Trust is the foundation of any healthy relationship, including friendships. Being reliable, keeping promises, and maintaining confidentiality can help build trust between friends.

Humor: Laughing together and sharing a good sense of humor can help lighten the mood and create positive memories with friends. Making your friends laugh is a great way to show them you care.

Supportiveness: Being there for your friends during challenging times and celebrating their successes is an essential part of any friendship.

Being supportive can help strengthen your bond and show your friends that you care.

Now that we know some of the essential friendship skills let's explore how developing these skills can be beneficial in the long run.

First and foremost, having strong friendship skills can help you build positive relationships with people throughout your life.

Whether it's in your personal or professional life, having the ability to connect with others, communicate effectively, and build trust can lead to many opportunities.

For example, having a network of friends who work in various fields can help you land your dream job, connect you to new business opportunities, or even introduce you to potential romantic partners.

Building friendships with people who have different backgrounds and experiences than you can help broaden your horizons and expand your worldview.

Moreover, strong friendship skills can lead to improved mental health and well-being.

When we have friends who support and encourage us, it can help reduce stress, increase self-esteem, and even improve our immune system.

Having positive social connections can also help us cope better with difficult situations and provide a sense of purpose and belonging.

Developing strong friendship skills is not only beneficial for building healthy and meaningful relationships with others, but it can also have a positive impact on our overall well-being and future opportunities.

So, let's work on honing our communication, empathy, and trustworthiness, humor, and supportiveness skills to build strong, lasting friendships that enrich our lives.

And remember, a good friend will always be there to make you laugh, even when you feel like crying.

Effective Communication Skills for You

Communication is a vital skill that every girl should possess.

Effective communication skills can be the difference between success and failure in various aspects of life, from school to relationships.

As girls, we are often taught to be polite and to avoid conflict. However, it's essential to know when and how to express ourselves to make sure we are understood and respected.

Here are some tips to help you become a better communicator:

Listen actively Effective: communication begins with listening. It's essential to listen actively, pay attention to what the other person is saying, and not just waiting for your turn to speak.

Listen to their tone, non-verbal cues, and try to understand their perspective. It's okay to ask questions and clarify things if you are not sure what they mean.

Speak clearly and confidently: When it's your turn to speak, speak clearly and confidently.

Use assertive language and avoid being passive or aggressive. It's okay to express your opinion and share your thoughts as long as you do it in a respectful and tactful way.

Use non-verbal cues: Your body language can convey a lot about your thoughts and emotions.

Pay attention to your posture, eye contact, and facial expressions. Try to be open and approachable, and avoid crossing your arms or looking away when you speak.

Practice empathy: Empathy is the ability to understand and share the feelings of another person. It's essential to put yourself in their shoes and try to see things from their perspective.

This skill will help you communicate more effectively and build better relationships.

Be mindful of your tone: Your tone of voice can have a significant impact on how your message is received.

Try to use a friendly and positive tone, even when discussing challenging topics. Avoid yelling or sounding aggressive, as this can make the other person defensive and less likely to listen.

Use humor: Humor can be a powerful tool in communication, but be mindful of the situation and the person you're speaking to.

A well-timed joke or a funny story can help break the ice and make the other person feel more comfortable.

By practicing these effective communication skills, you will be able to express yourself better, build stronger relationships, and achieve your goals.

Remember that communication is a two-way street, and it takes practice to become a great communicator. So, don't be afraid to speak up, listen carefully, and have fun!

Can I Have A Crush?

As a teenage girl, it's common to experience feelings of attraction or infatuation towards someone.

It could be someone in your class, a celebrity, or even a fictional character.

These feelings are perfectly normal, and we call them "crushes." However, the question arises, is having a crush a must? Do we need to have a crush to feel fulfilled or happy in life? Let's explore this topic and find out.

First of all, it's important to understand that having a crush is a natural part of growing up. It's a way for us to explore our feelings and desires, and it can be exciting and exhilarating.

Crushes can make us feel happy, nervous, and sometimes even a little bit silly.

But at the same time, we need to be careful not to let these feelings consume us or distract us from other important aspects of our lives.

It's essential to maintain a balance between our feelings and our responsibilities. For example, if you have a crush on someone, it's okay to spend time thinking about them or even daydreaming about them.

However, it's not okay to let your crush interfere with your schoolwork or your relationships with your family and friends.

Effective communication skills are crucial in managing our crushes. It's important to communicate our feelings and desires in a respectful and appropriate manner.

If you have a crush on someone, you can let them know how you feel, but you also need to be prepared to accept their response, whether it's positive or negative.

Remember that rejection is a normal part of life, and it doesn't define your worth as a person.

Moreover, it's important not to let your crush define your identity. You are more than just your feelings towards someone else.

You have your own unique personality, interests, and strengths that make you who you are. Don't try to change yourself to fit someone else's expectations or desires.

While having a crush can be fun and exciting, it's not necessary for a fulfilling life.

There are plenty of other things that can bring us joy and happiness, such as spending time with friends, pursuing our passions, or helping others.

It's essential to focus on these things and not let our crushes consume us.

In conclusion, having a crush is a normal part of growing up, but it's important to maintain a healthy balance between our feelings and our responsibilities.

Effective communication skills are essential in managing our crushes, and we should never let our crushes define our identities or consume us.

Remember to focus on the things that bring you joy and happiness, and you'll find that life can be fulfilling and exciting, with or without a crush.

Reading between the Lines: Body Language and Listening
Are you tired of feeling like you're missing something when you're talking to your friends?

Do you ever wonder if there's a deeper meaning behind what they're saying? Well, it's time to start paying attention to body language and listening skills!

Body language can tell you a lot about a person's feelings and intentions.

For example, if your friend is crossing their arms and avoiding eye contact, they may be feeling defensive or uncomfortable.

On the other hand, if they are leaning in and making eye contact, they are likely engaged and interested in the conversation.

But it's not just about what your friend's body is saying - it's also about what they're not saying.

Listening is a crucial skill in any relationship, and it involves more than just hearing the words that are spoken.

It's about paying attention to tone of voice, facial expressions, and even pauses in the conversation.

So, how can you improve your body language and listening skills? Here are a few tips:

Make eye contact: When you're talking to someone, make sure to look them in the eye. This shows that you are interested in what they have to say and that you are fully present in the conversation.

Smile: A smile is a universal sign of friendliness and happiness. A smile can make someone feel comfortable and at ease, and it can create a positive vibe. Smile genuinely, and avoid forcing it.

Avoid distractions: Put away your phone, turn off the TV, and focus on the conversation at hand. This not only shows respect for the other person, but it also helps you pick up on important cues in their body language and tone of voice.

Gestures: Your hand gestures can be powerful tools for communication. Use them to emphasize your point, but avoid overdoing it, as it can be distracting. Keep your gestures natural and relaxed.

Ask questions: Don't be afraid to ask clarifying questions or to dig deeper into what the other person is saying.

This not only shows that you are interested in what they have to say, but it also helps you understand their perspective better.

Practice active listening: Repeat back what the other person has said to you, or summarize their main points. This not only shows that you are paying attention, but it also helps ensure that you are both on the same page.

Listening: It's More Than Just Hearing

Listening is a crucial aspect of communication, and it involves more than just hearing. Here are some tips on how to be an active listener:

Pay Attention

Give the person speaking your undivided attention. Focus on what they are saying and avoid distractions such as your phone or other people around you.

Clarify

If you are unsure about something the person is saying, ask questions for clarification. It shows that you are interested in what they are saying and that you want to understand them better.

Empathize

Put yourself in the other person's shoes and try to understand their perspective. This shows that you are considerate and respectful of their feelings.

Respond

Respond appropriately to what the person is saying. It can be through words, nods, or even facial expressions. It shows that you are engaged in the conversation.

By improving your body language and listening skills, you can build stronger, more meaningful relationships with your friends.

So, next time you're having a conversation, pay attention to the cues your friend is giving off and make sure you're really listening to what they have to say!

Sure, here are a few case studies to illustrate the importance of good listening skills and effective communication:

Case Study 1: Sarah and her boss

Sarah is a new employee at a marketing agency. During her first week, she was given a task by her boss, John.

John gave Sarah a general outline of the task, but Sarah was unsure about some of the details.

However, she did not want to bother John with too many questions, as she did not want to seem incompetent.

As a result, Sarah spent several hours working on the task, but she did not produce the results that John was looking for.

When John reviewed Sarah's work, he realized that Sarah had not fully understood the task and had gone in the wrong direction.

In this case, Sarah's lack of effective communication and active listening skills caused her to waste valuable time and produce unsatisfactory results.

If she had asked John for clarification and actively listened to his instructions, she could have saved herself time and produced better work.

Case Study 2: Tom and his partner

Tom and his partner, Mark, have been together for several years. Lately, they have been arguing a lot and have been having trouble communicating with each other. Tom feels like Mark is not listening to him and does not understand his point of view.

One day, while they were having a heated argument, Tom realized that he was not effectively communicating his thoughts and feelings to Mark.

He was using accusatory language and not actively listening to Mark's side of the story.

Tom decided to take a step back and actively listen to Mark's point of view. He realized that Mark was feeling hurt and ignored, and that he needed more attention from Tom.

By actively listening and communicating effectively, Tom and Mark were able to work through their issues and strengthen their relationship.

In this case, Tom's effective communication and active listening skills helped him to understand Mark's perspective and work towards a resolution. If he had continued to use accusatory language and not actively listened, their relationship may have suffered further.

Case Study 3: Maria and her coworkers

Maria works in a busy office environment with several other coworkers.

Lately, Maria has been feeling overwhelmed and stressed with her workload. She has been struggling to keep up with her tasks and has been making mistakes.

One day, Maria's coworker, Rachel, noticed that Maria was struggling and asked if she needed any help. Maria initially declined, saying that she could handle it.

However, Rachel persisted and asked Maria to explain her workload and what tasks she needed help with.

Through active listening and effective communication, Rachel was able to help Maria prioritize her tasks and delegate some of her work to other coworkers.

This helped to reduce Maria's workload and alleviate her stress.

In this case, Rachel's effective communication and active listening skills helped her to identify a problem and offer a solution.

If she had not actively listened to Maria and communicated effectively, Maria's workload and stress may have continued to escalate.

Personal empowerment. It's a topic that sounds so...empowering. But what does it actually mean? And how can it help you in your everyday life?

Well, my young friend, personal empowerment is all about taking control of your life, and making choices that will lead you towards happiness and success.

It's about being confident in your abilities, standing up for yourself, and living life on your own terms.

Now, I know that might sound a bit daunting, but fear not! I'm here to give you some tips and tricks on how to become your own personal superhero. So, grab your cape and let's get started.

Be True to Yourself

The first step to personal empowerment is being true to yourself. This means recognizing your strengths and weaknesses, and accepting them for what they are.

It's about understanding your values and what's important to you, and staying true to those things no matter what.

For example, let's say you're a budding artist, but your parents want you to go to law school.

It can be tempting to cave in to their expectations and give up on your dreams, but true personal empowerment means standing up for what you believe in and pursuing your passions.

It might not be easy, but in the long run, it will lead to a more fulfilling life.

Set Goals

Another important aspect of personal empowerment is setting goals. This means figuring out what you want to achieve, and then creating a plan to get there. It could be something as simple as acing a math test, or as complex as starting your own business.

The key to setting goals is making them specific, measurable, and realistic. Instead of saying "I want to be rich," try saying "I want to save $500 by the end of the month." By making your goals concrete, you'll be more likely to achieve them.

Take Action

Of course, setting goals is just the first step. To truly become empowered, you need to take action.

This means putting in the time and effort to make your dreams a reality. It means practicing your craft, networking with others, and constantly learning and growing.

Your goal is to become a famous singer. You can't just sit around and wait for opportunities to come to you.

You need to practice your singing every day, take voice lessons, and perform at local venues to build up your experience and exposure.

Learn From Failure

Of course, not everything will go according to plan. There will be times when you fail, or things don't turn out the way you hoped.

But the key to personal empowerment is learning from those experiences, and using them to grow and improve.

Let's say you auditioned for a singing competition and didn't make it to the finals.

Instead of giving up, use that experience to figure out what you could have done better, and then use that knowledge to improve your singing for next time.

Surround Yourself with Positive People

Finally, one of the most important aspects of personal empowerment is surrounding yourself with positive people.

This means finding friends and mentors who support you, and who will encourage you to pursue your goals and dreams.

For example, if you want to become a famous singer, find a vocal coach who believes in you and can help you improve your skills.

Surround yourself with other aspiring musicians who can offer advice and support.

By surrounding yourself with positive influences, you'll be more likely to stay motivated and achieve your goals.

So there you have it, my young friend. Personal empowerment is all about being true to yourself, setting goals, taking action, learning from failure, and surrounding yourself with positive people.

By following these tips, you'll be well on your way to becoming your own personal superhero.

The Concept of Consent and Boundaries

Neglecting consent and boundaries can have serious consequences, especially for girls.

It can lead to a lack of respect for personal space and autonomy, resulting in a range of harmful behaviors such as sexual harassment, sexual assault, and even rape.

In fact, statistics show that 1 in 3 women will experience sexual violence in their lifetime, and the majority of these cases involve perpetrators known to the victim.

By not respecting consent and boundaries, individuals are essentially taking away a person's agency over their own body and actions.

This can lead to feelings of powerlessness, anxiety, and trauma for the victim.

It can also perpetuate a culture of sexual violence and harassment, where individuals believe that they are entitled to another person's body without their consent.

Neglecting consent and boundaries can also have long-term effects on mental health and well-being. Victims of sexual violence and harassment are more likely to experience depression, anxiety, and post-traumatic stress disorder (PTSD). They may also struggle with self-esteem and trust issues, and have difficulty forming healthy relationships.

One way to start teaching girls about consent and boundaries is to use age-appropriate language and scenarios.

For example, you could talk to younger girls about respecting personal space and asking for permission before giving hugs or touching someone else's belongings.

For older girls, you could have conversations about healthy relationships, the importance of communication and consent, and how to recognize and respond to red flags in relationships.

Neglecting consent and boundaries can have serious and long-lasting consequences for girls and women.

It's important to prioritize these topics in our conversations and education, and to empower girls to assert their boundaries and respect those of others.

By doing so, we can work towards creating a safer and more respectful society for everyone.

As a girl, it is important to learn about boundaries and consent in all aspects of life, including friendships, romantic relationships, and sexual encounters.

Understanding these concepts can help you build healthy relationships, foster self-respect, and protect yourself from harm. In this chapter, we will explore what boundaries and consent mean and why they are crucial.

BOUNDARIES: Boundaries refer to the limits that you set for yourself and others regarding what you are willing and not willing to do, say, or experience.

These boundaries can be physical, emotional, or sexual. It is important to be aware of your boundaries and to communicate them effectively to others.

For example, let's say you have a friend who is always borrowing your clothes without asking.

You may feel uncomfortable but not know how to address the issue.

Setting a boundary means communicating your feelings to your friend and letting them know that you would appreciate it if they asked for permission before borrowing your clothes.

CONSENT: Consent means giving permission or agreeing to something.

In the context of relationships and sexual encounters, it is crucial to obtain and respect consent.

It is important to understand that consent must be given freely and enthusiastically, and it can be withdrawn at any time.

Remember talking to your parents first is the best thing to do! REPEAT AFTER ME- I will talk to mum first if I need to give consent!

And also remember that romantic relationships can destroy your life and fill you with regrets almost forever when you get into it unprepared and at an early age.... Always wait! **THERE IS TIME FOR EVERYTHING!**

For example, let's say you are considering engaging in sexual activity with someone. You must obtain their clear and enthusiastic consent before proceeding.

Consent cannot be given if the person is under the influence of drugs or alcohol, or if they are unable to make rational decisions due to their mental state. It is also essential to respect the person's decision if they choose to withdraw their consent at any point.

THE IMPORTANCE OF BOUNDARIES AND CONSENT

Learning about boundaries and consent is critical for girls as they grow up and navigate relationships, whether it be with friends, family, or romantic partners.

Here are a few reasons why boundaries and consent are important:

Protecting Yourself: Boundaries and consent help you protect yourself from harm.

Setting boundaries helps you avoid situations that make you feel uncomfortable or unsafe.

Obtaining and respecting consent ensures that you are engaging in activities that you are comfortable with and have agreed to.

Building Healthy Relationships: Understanding boundaries and consent can help you build healthy relationships.

By setting and respecting boundaries, you are communicating your needs and expectations clearly, and this can lead to mutual respect and trust.

Similarly, obtaining and respecting consent in relationships can lead to positive experiences and build trust between partners.

Fostering Self-Respect: Knowing your boundaries and being able to communicate them effectively can help you foster self-respect. It shows that you value your needs and are not willing to compromise them for anyone. Similarly, respecting others' boundaries and obtaining their consent shows that you value their needs and respect them as individuals.

Understanding and practicing boundaries and consent are crucial for girls as they grow up and navigate relationships.

By doing so, you are empowering yourself and others to build healthy, respectful, and positive relationships.

CHAPTER FOUR

I DON'T LIKE HOME

Life at home can be a rollercoaster ride. From getting along with siblings to dealing with parents who may not always understand you, it can be a challenge to figure out what people want from you.

But fear not, because this chapter will explore some common situations and provide tips on how to handle them like a pro.

First, let's talk about siblings. Whether you have one or many, they can be a source of both love and frustration.

One moment you're laughing together and the next, you're arguing over who gets to use the bathroom first.

So, what do your siblings want from you? Well, they probably want your attention and affection, but they also want their own space and respect.

It's important to strike a balance between spending time together and giving each other some alone time.

And when conflicts arise, try to communicate calmly and respectfully to find a solution that works for everyone.

Next up, let's tackle the tricky subject of parents. You may feel like they want you to be the perfect child who always follows their rules and expectations.

But the truth is, they just want you to be happy and healthy.

Sometimes their way of showing it may come across as overbearing or strict, but it's important to remember that they're doing their best to guide you through life.

Of course, there will be times when you disagree with their decisions or feel like they don't understand you. In those moments, it's okay to express your feelings respectfully and have an open and honest conversation.

Now, let's move on to the topic of friends. What do they want from you? Well, they probably want your companionship, support, and a good time. But they also want you to be true to yourself and respect their boundaries.

It's important to listen to your friends and understand their perspectives, but it's equally important to stand up for yourself and communicate your own boundaries.

And if a friend is ever asking you to do something that makes you uncomfortable or goes against your values, it's okay to say no and prioritize your own well-being.

Finally, let's touch on the subject of romantic relationships. Whether you're crushing on someone or in a committed relationship, it's important to understand the importance of consent and respect for boundaries.

It's never okay for someone to pressure you into doing something you're not comfortable with, and it's important to communicate your boundaries clearly and confidently.

Remember, a healthy relationship is built on mutual respect, trust, and communication.

Navigating relationships at home can be challenging, but it's important to remember that everyone just wants to be happy and respected.

By communicating openly and respectfully, setting and respecting boundaries, and prioritizing your own well-being, you can create healthy and fulfilling relationships with your family, friends, and romantic partners.

I FEEL MY HOME IS NOT MINE!

Do you ever feel like you're living in a house full of strangers? Or like you're stuck in the same old routine with no hope of change?

Well, my dear reader, it's time to take control of your home life and start making some changes.

First and foremost, it's important to understand that change starts with you. You can't expect things to change if you keep doing the same old things.

So, take a good hard look at yourself and ask yourself what you can do to improve your home life.

One way to start is by communicating with your family members. Have a family meeting and discuss your concerns and ideas for making things better. It's important to listen to each other and respect each other's opinions. Remember, you're all in this together.

Another way to change things up is by trying new things together as a family. Maybe it's trying a new recipe for dinner or taking up a new hobby. Whatever it is, make sure it's something that everyone can enjoy and be a part of.

It's also important to create a positive environment at home. Avoid negativity and focus on the good things in life.

Celebrate each other's successes and lift each other up when times are tough. A little positivity can go a long way in creating a happy home life.

And lastly, don't be afraid to seek outside help if needed. Whether it's counseling or simply talking to a trusted friend or family member, sometimes it takes an outside perspective to help you see things in a different light.

Communicate, try new things, create a positive environment, and seek help when needed.

With a little effort and a lot of love, you can create a happy and fulfilling home life for yourself and your family.

Hey, home sweet home! It's where we feel comfortable and safe. But sometimes, it can feel like a prison, especially if you're stuck with family members who just don't understand you.

Maybe they're always nagging you to clean your room, or they're constantly in your business.

Whatever the case may be, it's important to remember that you have the power to change the atmosphere of your home.

It's natural to want to rebel against rules or expectations that feel stifling, but sometimes we forget that we can communicate our needs and desires in a respectful way.

It's all about finding the right balance between being assertive and compromising.

So, what can you do to change the dynamics of your home? Here are a few tips:

Start with yourself: It's important to recognize that changing the atmosphere of your home starts with changing yourself first.

Are you being respectful towards your family members?

Are you contributing positively to the household? Sometimes, a change in attitude can make all the difference.

Communicate effectively: Instead of getting angry or shutting down when you feel like your family is being overbearing, try to communicate your thoughts and feelings in a calm and respectful way.

This can mean sitting down with them and having an open and honest conversation about how you feel and what you need from them.

Find common ground: It's easy to get caught up in our own wants and needs, but it's important to remember that we're all living under the same roof.

Try to find common ground with your family members and work towards compromise.

Maybe you can agree on a cleaning schedule that works for everyone, or you can make a rule about knocking before entering each other's rooms.

Set boundaries: If you're feeling overwhelmed or suffocated, it's important to set boundaries. Do not completely shut everyone out!

Let your family members know what you're comfortable with and what you're not, and stick to it. It's okay to say "no" and prioritize your own mental health and well-being.

Here are a few examples of how she might put our tips into practice, with a little humor thrown in:

Decluttering: Jane decides to tackle her messy bedroom, following our advice to donate, sell, or toss anything she no longer needs or loves.

She's feeling pretty proud of herself until she discovers her little brother has taken over her discarded pile of clothes as a fort. "I guess that's one way to declutter," Jane muses as she surveys the chaos.

Rearranging furniture: Jane gets inspired by a home decor magazine and decides to rearrange the living room furniture to create a more inviting space for her family.

She enlists her dad's help, and together they move the couch to the opposite wall. "Wow, this really opens up the room," her dad says. "Now we can all fight over the best seat on the couch from any angle!"

Adding personal touches: Jane decides to display some of her favorite artwork and photos around the house, as we suggested.

She prints out some of her Instagram photos and frames them to create a gallery wall in her bedroom. When her mom sees the display, she exclaims, "I had no idea you were such a talented photographer!" Jane grins and replies, "Thanks, Mom. I'm available for hire if you need any family portraits!"

Bringing in nature: As we advised, Jane purchases some plants to bring some greenery to her house. In the kitchen, she creates a sweet small herb garden, and in the living room, she hangs some ferns.

"Cool, now we have a jungle in our house!" her younger sister says as soon as she notices the plants.

Watch careful for the lions and tigers, Jane chuckles in response.

Overall, Jane is pleased with the improvements she's made to her house, and her family seems to like the new vibe.

Although there could be a few jokes and hiccups along the way, remodeling your house can be a positive and enjoyable experience.

Keep in mind that changing your home's dynamics won't happen quickly. It requires tolerance, cognizance, and a desire to cooperate.

But with the correct mindset and strategy, you can establish a home setting that feels warm and encouraging.

Secret Agent Code Name: Mom

Are you tired of feeling like your mom is always watching your every move?

Do you sometimes wonder if she's secretly a spy, gathering intel on your every thought and action?

Well, fear not my friend, because I have a solution that will help you navigate your home life with ease and even have some fun doing it.

Step 1: Create a diversion

If you're feeling overwhelmed by your mom's watchful eye, create a diversion.

You can start by doing something that she doesn't expect, like suddenly breaking into a dance routine in the middle of the living room.

This will not only distract her, but it will also help you release some pent-up energy and have a good laugh in the process.

Step 2: Plant fake clues

If you suspect that your mom is snooping around your room, plant some fake clues to throw her off your scent.

For example, leave a note on your desk that says "Secret mission: watch paint dry." Your mom will think she's onto something big, but in reality, she's just wasting her time.

Step 3: Use spy lingo

If you really want to mess with your mom, start using spy lingo in your everyday conversations.

For instance, if your mom asks you what you did at school today, you can reply with something like, "I can neither confirm nor deny any activities that may or may not have occurred on the premises."

She'll either be impressed with your cleverness or completely confused, but either way, you'll have successfully thrown her off your trail.

Step 4: Enlist the help of allies

If all else fails, enlist the help of your siblings or friends to create a united front against your mom's surveillance tactics. You can start a secret club with a cool code name like "The Resistance" and come up with strategies to outsmart your mom together. Who knows, maybe she'll even be impressed with your cunning and recruit you for her own secret missions.

In all seriousness though, it's important to remember that your mom's actions come from a place of love and concern for your well-being.

While it may feel like she's invading your privacy at times, it's important to have open and honest communication with her about your boundaries and feelings.

With a little bit of humor and creativity, you can navigate your home life with ease and even have some fun doing it.

Chores and Wars

Ah, the chores. The source of all children's misery. However, whether you want to believe it or not, cleaning up after yourself can be beneficial.

In addition to keeping your living environment tidy and orderly, they can also help you learn responsibility, time management, and the value of cooperation.

I'm aware of your thoughts at this point. But work is so monotonous and uninteresting.

So don't worry, my young padawan. Even the most boring task can be made entertaining and pleasurable with the right attitude and a little imagination.

Let's take the scenario where you have the cleaning of the restroom as an example. Sounds tedious, don't you think? What if you made it into a game, though? See how quickly you can clean the shower, toilet, and sink by setting a timer for yourself.

Make it a contest between you and your siblings to see who can finish it the fastest. The task of cleaning the bathroom suddenly doesn't seem so bad.

Or perhaps you could wash the dishes? The worst, ugh. But what if, as you wipe away at those soiled plates, you put on some of your favorite music and had a dance party?

Even better, while cleaning up from supper, invite your siblings to join you in a family dance party. Who knew cleaning the dishes could be so enjoyable?

Also, don't forget about the laundry. It can be very tedious to sort, wash, and fold.

What if you made it a fashion show instead? As you fold, try on several costumes to see who can create the most original and fashionable look.

In the process, you might even come across a brand-new trend in clothing.

The point is that doing chores doesn't have to be dreadful. You may make them into an entertaining and delightful activity with a little imagination and a positive outlook.

Additionally, consider how proud you will be if your parents tell you that you did a good job.

So the next time you're given a task, resist the urge to moan and whine. Smile and take it in with a spirit of adventure. Who knows, you might even find that you have a knack for organizing and cleaning.

My First Friends are My Siblings

Sibling relationships may be an emotional rollercoaster. You can be best buddies one second and then be at each other's throats the next. It's all included in the price of having siblings.

What if I, however, were to inform you that being friends with your siblings is not only doable but also very rewarding?

You did read that correctly. Your life can be filled with so much happiness and fulfillment if you and your siblings get along well. It goes beyond simply sharing childhood memories and doing tasks together. It's about having a longtime friend that is completely familiar with you and will always have your back.

I'm aware of your thoughts at this point. "But my brother/sister annoys me so much!" or "How can we be friends when we don't have anything in common?" Don't worry, there are certain strategies that can help you establish a strong bond with your siblings.

Communication is crucial, to start. Regularly communicate with your siblings, even if it's only to chat.

As you inquire about their day and interests, pay close attention to their responses. By doing this, you demonstrate your concern for them and your interest in their life.

Second, discover areas of agreement. Regardless of your divergent interests, you two must share some common interests.

Find hobbies that you can do together and bond over, whether it be playing video games, watching movies, or taking a walk.

Third, be considerate of one another's boundaries. It's crucial to recognize and respect each other's personal boundaries and space in this friendship, just like in any other.

If your sibling is not comfortable doing anything, don't make them do it.

Last but not least, laugh and be funny together! One of the few people who can understand your peculiar sense of humor and inside jokes is probably your sibling. Accept your differences and have fun together.

Keep in mind that it takes time and work to develop a close bond with your siblings, but the benefits are worthwhile.

Along with a longtime friend, you'll also have someone who is familiar with the dynamics of your family and who can provide support and direction when you need it most.

Give your sibling a hug, let them know you appreciate them, and begin your friendship with them right away! They might even end up being your new favorite friend to spend out with, who knows?.

CONCLUSION

As we come to the end of this book, we hope that you have found it informative, helpful, and entertaining. Our goal was to provide practical tips, advice, and insights for girls as they navigate the complex and sometimes challenging journey of growing up.

We covered a wide range of topics, from self-care and managing emotions to making friends and communicating effectively. We also explored the dynamics of family relationships and how to set boundaries and respect consent.

Through humorous anecdotes, relatable examples, and practical strategies, we aimed to equip you with the tools you need to thrive in all areas of your life. Remember that growing up can be tough, but you are not alone. Reach out to trusted friends, family members, or professionals if you need support.

As you continue on your journey, keep in mind that self-love, self-respect, and self-care are essential. Always prioritize your well-being and listen to your intuition. You are capable of achieving great things and living a fulfilling life, and we believe in you.

Thank you for joining us on this journey, and we wish you all the best in your future endeavors.